The ATTRIBUTES *of* GOD

KRISTIN SCHMUCKER

Study Suggestions

We believe that the Bible is true, trustworthy, and timeless and that it is vitally important for all believers. These study suggestions are intended to help you more effectively study Scripture as you seek to know and love God through His Word.

SUGGESTED STUDY TOOLS

A Bible

A double-spaced, printed copy of the Scripture passages that this study covers. You can use a website like *www.biblegateway.com* to copy the text of a passage and print out a double-spaced copy to be able to mark on easily

A journal to write notes or prayers

Pens, colored pencils, and highlighters

A dictionary to look up unfamiliar words

HOW TO USE THIS STUDY

Begin your study time in prayer. Ask God to reveal Himself to you, to help you understand what you are reading, and to transform you with His Word (Psalm 119:18).

Before you read what is written in each day of the study itself, read the assigned passages of Scripture for that day. Use your double-spaced copy to circle, underline, highlight, draw arrows, and mark in any way you would like to help you dig deeper as you work through a passage.

Read the daily written content provided for the current study day.

Answer the questions that appear at the end of each study day.

HOW TO STUDY THE BIBLE

The inductive method provides tools for deeper and more intentional Bible study. To study the Bible inductively, work through the steps below after reading background information on the book.

1 **OBSERVATION & COMPREHENSION**
Key question: What does the text say?

After reading the daily Scripture in its entirety at least once, begin working with smaller portions of the Scripture. Read a passage of Scripture repetitively, and then mark the following items in the text:

- Key or repeated words and ideas
- Key themes
- Transition words (Ex: therefore, but, because, if/then, likewise, etc.)
- Lists
- Comparisons & Contrasts
- Commands
- Unfamiliar words (look these up in a dictionary)
- Questions you have about the text

2 **INTERPRETATION**
Key question: What does the text mean?

Once you have annotated the text, work through the following steps to help you interpret its meaning:

- Read the passage in other versions for a better understanding of the text.
- Read cross-references to help interpret Scripture with Scripture.
- Paraphrase or summarize the passage to check for understanding.
- Identify how the text reflects the metanarrative of Scripture, which is the story of creation, fall, redemption, and restoration.
- Read trustworthy commentaries if you need further insight into the meaning of the passage.

3. APPLICATION
Key Question: How should the truth of this passage change me?

Bible study is not merely an intellectual pursuit. The truths about God, ourselves, and the gospel that we discover in Scripture should produce transformation in our hearts and lives. Answer the following questions as you consider what you have learned in your study:

- What attributes of God's character are revealed in the passage?

    Consider places where the text directly states the character of God, as well as how His character is revealed through His words and actions.

- What do I learn about myself in light of who God is?

    Consider how you fall short of God's character, how the text reveals your sin nature, and what it says about your new identity in Christ.

- How should this truth change me?

    A passage of Scripture may contain direct commands telling us what to do or warnings about sins to avoid in order to help us grow in holiness. Other times our application flows out of seeing ourselves in light of God's character. As we pray and reflect on how God is calling us to change in light of His Word, we should be asking questions like, "How should I pray for God to change my heart?" and "What practical steps can I take toward cultivating habits of holiness?"

METANARRATIVE OF SCRIPTURE

Creation

In the beginning, God created the universe. He made the world and everything in it. He created humans in His own image to be His representatives on the earth.

Fall

The first humans, Adam and Eve, disobeyed God by eating from the fruit of the Tree of Knowledge of Good and Evil. Because of sin, the world was cursed. The punishment for sin is death, and because of Adam's original sin, all humans are sinful and condemned to death.

Redemption

God sent his Son to become a human and redeem His people. Jesus Christ lived a sinless life but died on the cross to pay the penalty for sin. He resurrected from the dead and ascended into heaven. All who put their faith in Jesus are saved from death and freely receive the gift of eternal life.

Restoration

One day, Jesus Christ will return again and restore all that sin destroyed. He will usher in a new heaven and new earth where all who trust in Him will live eternally with glorified bodies in the presence of God.

We were *made to know God*, and we were *made to reflect His image* to the world around us.

in this study

WEEK ONE

Day 1: Introduction	11
Extra: The Attributes of God Chart	12
Day 2: Who Is God?	17
Day 3: Knowing God	21
Day 4: The Character of God and Bible Study	25
Extra: Psalm 119	29
Day 5: Communicable and Incommunicable	31
Extra: Communicable and Incommunicable Attributes	34
Day 6: Scripture Memory Jeremiah 9:24	37
Day 7: Weekly Reflection	38

WEEK 2

Day 1: Eternal	41
Day 2: Infinite	45
Day 3: Immutable	49
Day 4: Self-Existent	53
Day 5: Self-Sufficient	57
Extra: "I Need Thee Every Hour"	60
Day 6: Scripture Memory Jeremiah 10:6	63
Day 7: Weekly Reflection	64

WEEK 3

Day 1: Omnipresent	67
Day 2: Omniscient	71
Day 3: Omnipotent	75
Day 4: Incomprehensible and Transcendent	79
Day 5: Sovereign	83
Day 6: Scripture Memory Exodus 34:6	87
Day 7: Weekly Reflection	88
Extra: Communicable Attributes	91

WEEK 4

Day 1: Holy	93
Day 2: Loving	97
Day 3: Good	101
Day 4: Truthful	105
Day 5: Just	109
Day 6: Scripture Memory Psalm 145:3	113
Day 7: Weekly Reflection	114

WEEK 5

Day 1: Wrathful	117
Extra: Misunderstanding God's Wrath	*121*
Day 2: Merciful	123
Day 3: Gracious	127
Day 4: Jealous	131
Day 5: Patient	135
Day 6: Scripture Memory 2 Peter 3:18	139
Day 7: Weekly Reflection	140

WEEK 6

Day 1: Wise	143
Day 2: Faithful	147
Day 3: How We Can Know God	151
Day 4: Knowing Him and Being Known By Him	155
Day 5: Reflecting God's Attributes	159
Day 6: Scripture Memory Psalm 86:11	163
Day 7: Weekly Reflection	164

ADDITIONAL RESOURCES

Attributes of God Scripture Reference Guide	*167*
What is the Gospel?	*172*

We study God's attributes to *know Him*.

WEEK ONE *day one*

"
A right understanding of *who God is* gives our faith a foundation to *rest upon*.
"

Introduction

Read Jeremiah 9:23-24, Psalm 27:8

Knowing God is foundational to the Christian life. Our walk with God will not progress if we do not grow in our knowledge of God. Yet, in our time, we are far more likely to see self-help books lining the shelves than books exploring who God is. We are a culture obsessed with ourselves. Many of us have taken every personality test we can find in an attempt to understand ourselves. But what if the best measure for knowing who we are is to know who God is? What if we stopped trying to make God just like us and started to see how He has called us to become more like Him?

How we view God impacts how we view everything, and our struggles and sin are rooted in a wrong view of God. It is no coincidence that at the dawn of creation, Satan sought to make Eve question who God is and what He said. If the enemy can convince us that God is not who He says that He is, we can easily fall into temptation. A right understanding of who God is gives our faith a foundation to rest upon. Knowing God draws us into an intimate relationship with Him that enables us to flee sin and run to the arms of our Savior. And one of the ways to know God is to study and understand His attributes.

The attributes of God reveal three things. They reveal His character, our sin, and the glorious gospel. Over the next six weeks, we will slowly walk through 22 attributes of God. We will see the ways in which God is totally different from us, and we will also see the ways that we are called to become more like Him. We will see that God can be known. He has revealed Himself in His Word and is revealing Himself even now by His Spirit. If we want to grow in grace, we must grow in our knowledge of who God is. Understanding who He is puts every aspect of our life and the world into perspective.

As you begin this study, pray that you would know God more today than yesterday. May this be your prayer every day of your life.

The Attributes of God

ETERNAL
God has no beginning and no end. He always was, always is, and always will be.

HAB. 1:12 / REV. 1:8 / IS. 41:4

FAITHFUL
God is incapable of anything but fidelity. He is loyally devoted to His plan and purpose.

2 TIM. 2:13 / DEUT. 7:9
HEB. 10:23

GOOD
God is pure; there is no defilement in Him. He is unable to sin, and all He does is good.

GEN. 1:31 / PS. 34:8 / PS. 107:1

GRACIOUS
God is kind, giving us gifts and benefits we do not deserve.

2 KINGS 13:23 / PS. 145:8
IS. 30:18

HOLY
God is undefiled and unable to be in the presence of defilement. He is sacred and set-apart.

REV. 4:8 / LEV. 19:2 / HAB. 1:13

INCOMPREHENSIBLE & TRANSCENDENT
God is high above and beyond human understanding. He is unable to be fully known.

PS. 145:3 / IS. 55:8-9
ROM. 11:33-36

IMMUTABLE
God does not change. He is the same yesterday, today, and tomorrow.

1 SAM. 15:29 / ROM. 11:29
JAMES 1:17

INFINITE
God is limitless. He exhibits all of his attributes perfectly and boundlessly.

ROM. 11:33-36 / IS. 40:28
PS. 147:5

JEALOUS
God is desirous of receiving the praise and affection He rightly deserves.

EX. 20:5 / DEUT. 4:23-24
JOSH. 24:19

JUST
God governs in perfect justice. He acts in accordance with justice. In Him, there is no wrongdoing or dishonesty.

IS. 61:8 / DEUT. 32:4 / PS. 146:7-9

LOVING
God is eternally, enduringly, steadfastly loving and affectionate. He does not forsake or betray His covenant love.

JN. 3:16 / EPH. 2:4-5 / 1 JN. 4:16

MERCIFUL
God is compassionate, withholding from us the wrath that we deserve.

TITUS 3:5 / PS. 25:10
LAM. 3:22-23

OMNIPOTENT
God is all-powerful; His strength is unlimited.

MAT. 19:26 / JOB 42:1-2
JER. 32:27

OMNIPRESENT
God is everywhere; His presence is near and permeating.

PROV. 15:3 / PS. 139:7-10
JER. 23:23-24

OMNISCIENT
God is all-knowing; there is nothing unknown to Him.

PS. 147:4 / I JN. 3:20
HEB. 4:13

PATIENT
God is long-suffering and enduring. He gives ample opportunity for people to turn toward Him.

ROM. 2:4 / 2 PET. 3:9 / PS. 86:15

SELF-EXISTENT
God was not created but exists by His power alone.

PS. 90:1-2 / JN. 1:4 / JN. 5:26

SELF-SUFFICIENT
God has no needs and depends on nothing, but everything depends on God.

IS. 40:28-31 / ACTS 17:24-25
PHIL. 4:19

SOVEREIGN
God governs over all things; He is in complete control.

COL. 1:17 / PS. 24:1-2
1 CHRON. 29:11-12

TRUTHFUL
God is our measurement of what is fact. By Him are we able to discern true and false.

JN. 3:33 / ROM. 1:25 / JN. 14:6

WISE
God is infinitely knowledgeable and is judicious with His knowledge.

IS. 46:9-10 / IS. 55:9 / PROV. 3:19

WRATHFUL
God stands in opposition to all that is evil. He enacts judgment according to His holiness, righteousness, and justice.

PS. 69:24 / JN. 3:36 / ROM. 1:18

Pray that you would know God *more today* than yesterday.

day one QUESTIONS

What attributes come to mind when you think about the attributes of God?

What attributes of God have brought you the most comfort?

Write out a prayer asking God to help you know Him more through His Word during this study.

"Our *view of God* shapes our view of *everything* else."

Who is God?

Read Psalm 86:5-12

Who is God? This question must be answered before we can begin to look at the attributes of God. The Bible is a book about God. It is a book that points the reader to who He is. It points to His attributes and tells of His works. Our view of God matters. A. W. Tozer famously wrote that "What comes into our mind when we think about God is the most important thing about us." Our view of God shapes our view of everything else. We interpret every aspect of our lives based on our understanding of who God is. Therefore, the way we view Him is immensely important. Our view of God is foundational to our worldview. And not only that, but it impacts the way we live day to day and moment by moment.

Yet, many are not sure who God is. In fact, there is a tendency for humanity to imagine God in a way that pleases them. Some think of God as a sort of universal police officer who does not want anyone to have any fun. This view of God makes people think that, at His core, God is not truly good. To those who take this view, it seems that God is out to get everyone. This view of God makes Him seem untrustworthy and suspect. But this is not who God is. Others view God as a grandfatherly figure. He is a kind of Santa Claus who is kind to everyone. He is not bothered by our sin and would be pleased if we just tried our best to be nice humans. But this is not God.

The Bible paints a far different picture of who God is. The story of Scripture declares who God is. The Bible reveals His character by describing who He is as well as presenting His actions. The same Bible that declares that God is love demonstrates this love by recounting God's works of steadfast love through all of time. The opening pages of Scripture point to God as the Creator and source of all things (Genesis 1). The world continues only by His sustaining hand. Scripture declares God to be one God revealed to us in three persons. The mystery of the Trinity is central to who God is, and every attribute of God is true of each person of the Trinity (John 5:17-19). Scripture declares to us that God is not silent. He is a God who speaks (Isaiah 55:11). He calls His own out of every tribe, tongue, and nation (Revelation 5:9). His love is steadfast and sure (Lamentations 3:22-23), and He is faithful even when His children chase after the pleasures of this world (2 Timothy 2:13). He is a God who draws near and longs to dwell with His people (Exodus 29:45, Ezekiel 37:27), a truth displayed throughout Scripture but evidenced most fully in the incarnation of Jesus (John 1:14). God Himself became a man to draw near to His own. He humbled Himself as a man without losing an ounce of His deity. Every attribute of God is perfectly revealed in Jesus Christ. He is a God who calls His own to follow Him (John 10:27). He is a God who indwells and empowers His children to answer His call (John 16:7). He is a God who is working even now (Philippians 1:6). He is a God who is coming again (Acts 1:11).

The Bible is a book about God, and every single verse declares His attributes. Sometimes with a shout and sometimes in a whisper, the Bible is telling us who God is. In our own lives, the Spirit reveals God to us in much the same way, from the shouting glory of a majestic sunset that points us to Him to the whisper of the Spirit's comfort. And though we can see His glory all around us, it is within the pages of His Word that we come to know Him.

As the people of God, our greatest desire should be to know Him more and bring glory to His name. We should desire to know God so fully that our hearts are aligned to His heart. That is what this study is about: learning the heart of God so that we can align our hearts with His. We are not seeking mere academic knowledge of who He is. We are seeking to be transformed by the intimate knowledge of our God. We are seeking to have hearts that beat for what His heart beats for. We are seeking to be transformed into His image, moment by ordinary moment. We are seeking a knowledge of God that is far more than surface Christianity. We are seeking to know God and be known by Him.

We should desire to know God so fully that our hearts are aligned to His heart.

How do you describe who God is?

How do you think your view of God changes the way that you see the world?

How do you think your daily life would change if you knew God more deeply?

day two QUESTIONS

WEEK ONE *day three*

"*Knowing* God and *glorifying* Him is what we were created for."

Knowing God

Read Philippians 3:7-10

What does it mean to know God? Knowing God has become a bit of a cliché in Christian culture. Many people talk about knowing Him, but how many of us can truly say that we know Him deeply and intimately? Our goal in this study is to get past the clichés when it comes to talking about who God is and knowing Him. Instead, we want to know God. We want to truly, deeply, and intimately know Him. Because knowing God and glorifying Him is what we were created for.

Many people know about God—whether believers or unbelievers—but knowing God is so much more than knowing about Him. Knowing God is more than an academic knowledge of what the Bible says. We can be theologians who know all the right answers without knowing God deeply. This truth should be a wake-up call for every person who loves theology and studying God's Word. Theology is not the enemy. When viewed or studied correctly, theology should only encourage a greater love and affection for Christ. But if theology is divorced from the intimate knowledge of God, we have a problem.

Knowing God is also not just an experience. It is not an emotional high or a spiritual event. Instead, it is a relationship that is built little by little over time. In Philippians 3, Paul speaks about knowing Christ. He says that he counts everything as loss compared to knowing Christ. To Paul, as it should be to all disciples, knowing Christ was of the utmost importance. Everything else in life pales in comparison. Can we truly say that we would rather know Christ and lose everything than have all the things that this world offers but not know Jesus? Paul says that knowing Christ is of "surpassing value" (Philippians 3:8). There is nothing that compares to knowing Him.

Knowing God makes our hearts passionate about the mission of God. As we know God more, our hearts align with His heart, and our greatest desire becomes to live with our lives as an offering for His service. To live as an offering means to give ourselves up to God so that He can do His will with us. Furthermore, knowing Him gives fuel to our faith and propels us to action. When we truly know God, it is manifested in our obedience to God. 1 John 2:4 reminds us that we are liars if we say that we know Him but do not do what He says. Our obedience to the God we know and love demonstrates true faith and true knowledge of God.

Knowing God also changes the way we think about God, Scripture, our lives, and the world around us. It teaches us to interpret our lives and the world around us in light of what we know to be true about God. We are often tempted to change our view of who God is based on our experience, but knowing God changes our perspective. It sets our perspective in line with His perspective. Knowing God is reflected in our contentment with the life that God has given to us. Discontentment is—at its root—an accusation against God's character. Discontentment says that God has not given us all we need. But when we truly know the goodness of God, we will not doubt His sovereign will in our life circumstances (Philippians 4:11-13).

Knowing God means that we have a place to run when life does not make sense. It means that we have a friend who "sticks closer than a brother" (Proverbs 18:24). Nothing in this life is more important than knowing and being known by God (1 Corinthians 8:3).

So as we prepare to look closely at the attributes and character of God, may it be our great desire to go beyond knowing about God and grow in knowing Him more deeply.

Nothing in this life is more important than knowing and being known by God.

What is the difference between knowing about God and knowing God?

What did you learn from today's passage about knowing God?

Take a moment to prayerfully assess your relationship with God. Write out a prayer below, asking God to help you know Him more.

day three QUESTIONS

> *The more that we know Him,* the more we will long to know Him better.

The Character Of God and Bible Study

Read Psalm 119

The most important question we can ask as we study the Bible is, "What does this teach me about God?" The Bible is a book about God, but it is easy to forget that fact as we open its pages. We may be tempted to look to it for a quick fix for our current situation or view it as an academic textbook. But when we begin to understand that the purpose of God's Word is far more significant than quick fixes and academics, we are freed to see Scripture as a channel for helping us to know our God.

God's character and attributes are on display in Scripture from Genesis to Revelation. Each book, chapter, and verse tells us who He is and how He works in this world. As we open our Bibles, we learn who God is. Sometimes God's character is explicitly stated in the text by telling us of His goodness, faithfulness, or some other aspect of who He is. Other times, we must discern God's attributes by observing what God does and how He interacts with man. We can see His faithfulness to His promises in the lives of His people. In this study, we will look deeply at the attributes of God. One of the greatest rewards of studying God's attributes is that in having a deeper understanding of who God is, we can begin to see His character more and more in the pages of God's Word.

In simple terms, it is a little like when you purchase a new or used vehicle and experience the strange phenomenon of suddenly seeing that model of car everywhere you go. Something that weeks before you may not have noticed on the road, now stands out to you at every intersection, school pick-up line, and store parking lot. This happens because your knowledge of this thing has made it stand out to you. This is the goal of studying God's character in Scripture. As we know who God is, His attributes will begin to jump off of the pages of the Bible. Suddenly the things we may not have noticed before stand out to us as we read God's Word.

The more that we know Him, the more we will long to know Him better. This is what

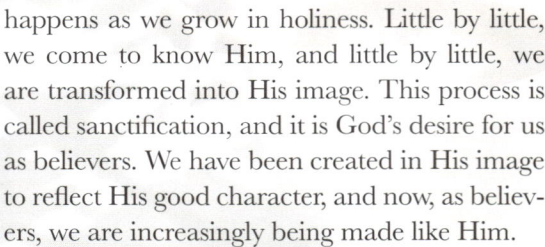

happens as we grow in holiness. Little by little, we come to know Him, and little by little, we are transformed into His image. This process is called sanctification, and it is God's desire for us as believers. We have been created in His image to reflect His good character, and now, as believers, we are increasingly being made like Him.

So we study God's Word to know Him more — not just to know about Him but to truly and deeply know Him. Knowing God is the key to knowing the Bible, and knowing the Bible is the key to knowing God. Knowing God is not something that we can simply cross off a checklist. And it is not something that we can ultimately achieve. We do not receive a degree in knowing God. But as we seek Him through His Word, we will grow in our love and knowledge of Him. And as we grow in our knowledge of Him, we will grow in our love and knowledge of His Word. The knowledge of God and the knowledge of His Word are intended to go together.

The idea of growing in our love and knowledge of God and His Word is nothing new. For example, the author of Psalm 119 praises God's character and His Word. In each of the 22 sections in the psalm, the psalmist proclaims that as he delights in and meditates on God's Word, God's character is revealed. Specifically, Psalm 119:65-68 clearly shows this idea. In these verses, the psalmist connects how the knowledge of God's Word has expanded his knowledge of God's character as he writes, "Lord, you have treated your servant well, just as you promised. Teach me good judgment and discernment, for I rely on your commands. Before I was afflicted I went astray, but now I keep your word. You are good, and you do what is good; teach me your statutes."

The psalmist shows us that keeping God's Word brings us close to Him and reveals God's character to us — in the case of this psalm, His Word reveals that God is faithful and good. We share Psalm 119 with you so that you can refer back to it during this study to be reminded of who God is and how His character is revealed in His Word.

As we open the Word of God, may our hearts be turned to the face of God. May we seek to know who He is, what He does, and His heart for us.

Knowing God is the key to knowing the Bible, and knowing the Bible is the key to knowing God.

What themes stand out to you as you read Psalm 119?

Why are God's character and attributes such an important part of Bible study?

How does reading Scripture to know God change our perspective on Scripture?

day four QUESTIONS

Psalm 119

Psalm 119 is a powerful chapter that demonstrates how studying God's Word reveals His character. We have included a portion of this Psalm 119 here. Bookmark this page, and return to it as you complete this study so that you can be reminded of who God is and how His Word reveals His character.

PSALM 119:65-72

Lord, you have treated your servant well,
just as you promised.
Teach me good judgment and discernment,
for I rely on your commands.
Before I was afflicted I went astray,
but now I keep your word.
You are good, and you do what is good;
teach me your statutes.
The arrogant have smeared me with lies,
but I obey your precepts with all my heart.
Their hearts are hard and insensitive,
but I delight in your instruction.
It was good for me to be afflicted
so that I could learn your statutes.
Instruction from your lips is better for me
than thousands of gold and silver pieces.

WEEK ONE *day five*

"We look to the *example of Jesus* to teach us how to live."

Communicable and Incommunicable Attributes

Read Genesis 1:27, Jeremiah 10:6, Hebrews 1:1-3

All people are made in the image of God. We bear His imprint and are made to reflect His glory. Through the process of sanctification, we are progressively growing in how we reflect and embody that image. Scripture abounds with a call for God's people to be holy as He is holy. And yet, there are many ways that we will never be like God because we are not God. There are attributes of God that are only true of God and will only ever be true of God.

Theologians typically group God's attributes into two categories, most often called the communicable and incommunicable attributes of God. God's communicable attributes are those attributes that humans can also possess, though not in the same way that God does. An example of a communicable attribute is love. Though God is perfectly loving, humans can imperfectly reflect this attribute of God. Believing and unbelieving people may love their children, spouses, or neighbors. God is the ultimate example of what love is, but He has enabled humans to share this quality. When we love, we reveal that we are made in the image of God.

The incommunicable attributes are those that cannot be true of any human. These are things that describe God alone. An example of an incommunicable attribute is omniscience. Omniscience tells us that God is all-knowing. No matter how hard we try as humans, we will never be omniscient. No matter how much we seek to learn and understand, we will never know all things. This characteristic is reserved for God alone. The incommunicable attributes remind us that God is different from us, and this distinction is for our good. We were never made to be gods of our own lives. We need the Lord.

We must look to Jesus as our perfect example of what it means to live out the communicable attributes of God. Jesus took on flesh, showing us what it means for humanity to reflect the image of God. It is in Jesus that we see the face of God. It is in

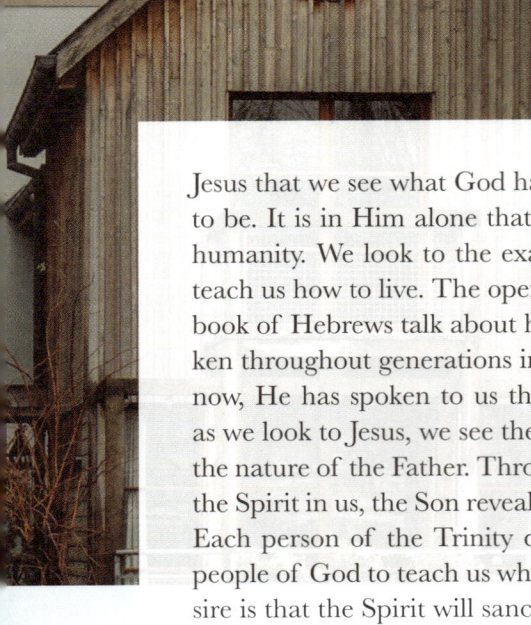

Jesus that we see what God has designed for us to be. It is in Him alone that we see perfected humanity. We look to the example of Jesus to teach us how to live. The opening verses of the book of Hebrews talk about how God has spoken throughout generations in many ways. But now, He has spoken to us through Jesus. And as we look to Jesus, we see the exact imprint of the nature of the Father. Through the power of the Spirit in us, the Son reveals the Father to us. Each person of the Trinity draws near to the people of God to teach us who God is. Our desire is that the Spirit will sanctify us, making us more and more holy, so that we rightly display the image of the Father, Son, and Spirit in our lives. We are His people. We bear His image, and He knows us by name. He has called us His own, and now, He calls us holy.

In this study, we will look at both the incommunicable and the communicable attributes of God. We will seek to know God, even as we are fully known by Him. We will worship God for who He is and respond in adoration by His grace. We will prayerfully ask God to change us and help us better reflect His image to the world around us.

We must look to Jesus as our perfect example of what it means to live out the communicable attributes of God.

Read the list of communicable and incommunicable attributes on the next page. In which communicable attributes do you think you most need to grow?

Which incommunicable attribute is hardest for you to comprehend?

Which communicable attributes do you find yourself desiring?

day five QUESTIONS

Communicable Attributes

Holy

Loving

Good

Just

Wrathful

Merciful

Gracious

Jealous

Patient

Wise

Faithful

Incommunicable Attributes

Eternal

Infinite

Immutable

Self-Existent

Self-Sufficient

Omnipresent

Omniscient

Omnipotent

Incomprehensible & Transcendent

Sovereign

WEEK ONE
Scripture Memory

But the one who boasts should boast in this: that he understands and knows me—that I am the Lord, showing faithful love, justice, and righteousness on the earth, for I delight in these things. This is the Lord's declaration.

—

JEREMIAH 9:24

week one REFLECTION
Review all passages from the week

Summarize the main points from this week's Scripture readings.

What did you observe from this week's passages about God and His character?

What do this week's passages reveal about the condition of mankind and yourself?

How do these passages point to the gospel?

How should you respond to these Scriptures? What specific action steps can you take this week to apply them in your life?

Write a prayer in response to your study of God's Word. Adore God for who He is, confess sins He revealed in your own life, ask Him to empower you to walk in obedience, and pray for anyone who comes to mind as you study.

WEEK TWO *day one*

> He holds *each moment* of our days in His hands.

Eternal

Read Isaiah 46:9-10, Revelation 1:4, 8, Hebrews 13:8, Psalm 90

God is eternal. He has no beginning and no end. He has always been, and He will always be. He is not bound by time. Instead, He holds time in the palm of His hand. He is altogether different than we are as finite creatures. Moses declares in the psalms that the Lord is from everlasting to everlasting. The book of Revelation tells us that He is Alpha and Omega, the beginning and the end. The Bible itself starts with the words "In the beginning," yet God existed long before our world began. All things were created by the One who was not created. There is no beginning or end to who He is. He simply is. As the Lord spoke to Moses so long ago, He is the I AM (Exodus 3:14-15).

These things are far outside the scope of our understanding. We have no concept of what it means to be eternal because we are not. We have a date of birth, and we will have a date of death. We have a limited perspective of time because we live in this time, in this year, in this decade, in this generation. The eternality of God is foundational to who He is. When we speak of the attributes of God, we speak of God being always good, loving, just, etc. Without the eternality of God, we cannot say "always." But because He is eternal, we can speak of God's attributes in conjunction with God's eternality. He is eternally good, loving, just, etc.

God is outside of time, and yet He meets us in time. He enters into our reality to dwell with us. This is most fully evidenced to us through the incarnation of Jesus, who took on the limitations of humanity to dwell with us. We can find great comfort that God exists outside of time. His perspective is far different than ours is. All we can see is the here and now. We often cannot even fathom how God is working in our circumstances. What we see as hopeless, God sees from an eternal perspective, and He is our hope. He knows where we have been, and He knows what is ahead. As humans, we do not know what the future holds, and we often cannot make sense of the past, yet we can rest in the eternal God who is never caught off guard. He holds each moment of our days in His hands (Psalm 31:15 ESV).

We take comfort in the God who is the same yesterday, today, and forever. We rest in the knowledge that He who is eternal meets us in our moments. We are not eternal, but we were made for eternity. We have a definite beginning, and through the power of the gospel, we are given eternal life in Christ (John 5:24). Our bodies will die, but we will live. When Jesus returns, we who believe in Him will receive glorified, resurrected bodies that will never fade away (1 John 3:2, Philippians 3:21). This is the power of the resurrected Jesus. He has conquered death for us and gives His children life that will not end.

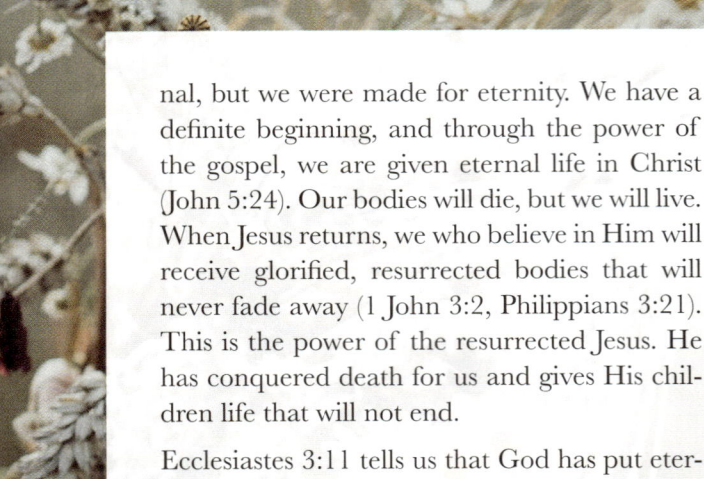

Ecclesiastes 3:11 tells us that God has put eternity in our hearts. He has created us to live for things that last forever. We are tempted by things that do not last. We are tempted to run to things that are not eternal for satisfaction, affirmation, and fulfillment. We run to sex, wine, food, approval, body image, another Amazon Prime order, and so many other things. But temporal things will never satisfy a heart that has been made to feast on the eternal. The eternal God is the only one who will satisfy the longings of our hearts (Psalm 107:9).

So "teach us to number our days." This is what Moses prays in Psalm 90, the glorious psalm about the eternal God. The eternality of God should teach us to live out our days well. It should remind us of our limitations and propel us to adore the God who is not limited. God is calling us to live for eternity. We must find our joy in the eternal God and not the temporary pleasures of this world. The psalmist continues to say that as we are taught to number our days, we "develop wisdom in our hearts." We need the wisdom of God to number our days well. We need the wisdom of God to live for the things that matter for eternity and to help us look to Him for satisfaction. And James so perfectly reminds us that if we ask Him for wisdom, He will give it (James 1:5). May we worship our eternal God, trust Him for each moment, and learn to live for what truly matters.

Temporal things will never satisfy a heart that has been made to feast on the eternal.

What does it mean that God is eternal? Why is that a good thing?

What are some of the temporary things that you look to for satisfaction? How is God better than these things?

How can you number your days? What would you change about your life if you live with eternity in view?

WEEK TWO *day two*

> "
> We were not made to be *limitless*; we were made to worship a *limitless* God.
> "

Infinite

Read Romans 11:33-36, Isaiah 40:28, Psalm 147:5, 2 Corinthians 12:9-10

God is infinite. He is limitless and far above our comprehension. It is hard for us as finite creatures even to grasp what infinite is. Perhaps as children, we used phrases like "…times infinity" to show the depth of our love or to win an argument with another child. In using the word "infinity" in this way, we present it as the pinnacle of something. Infinity is the answer that a child gives when asked how much he loves his mom or how much he hates his vegetables. In many ways, our greatest grasp on infinity is that it is a lot, and we struggle for words when we try to understand what it means in relation to God.

God is the only infinite one. The infinity of God is an incommunicable attribute and is something that God alone possesses. This attribute of God shares some similarities with eternity in that it can be used to describe God's other attributes. God is infinitely wise, just, loving, gracious, etc. In addition, God is perfect in all of His attributes as He is the very definition of what these attributes are. He is the standard against which all things are held. God is also infinite in time. He has no beginning, and He has no end. Though the pages of Genesis 1 record the beginning of the world for us, the God of Heaven has no beginning, no origin, and no creator. God is also infinite in space. This ties closely to the omnipresence—the ability to be everywhere simultaneously—of the Lord. He is not limited by the laws of gravity or to a single location. He transcends all things, yet He draws near to us. He is far more than we could ever comprehend.

We are the opposite of infinite. We are finite beings and are limited in every area of life. Our sinful natures often cause us to seek infinity in our own lives, but we were never meant to embody this characteristic of God. In our pursuit of being infinite, we reject our limitations, take on too many responsibilities, and refuse the rest that God requires of us. We are frustrated by our limitations as well as the limitations of others. But we are finite and limited creatures. We have a beginning, and our lives on this earth will have an end. We are not God.

But this is good news for us. We were not made to be gods; we were made to worship God. We were not made to be limitless; we were made to worship a limitless God. We were not made to be ultimate but to point to the ultimate One. The recognition that we are not infinite allows us to boast not in ourselves but in the limitless strength of God in us (2 Corinthians 12:9-10). Our weakness reminds us of who God is. Our weakness is a gift to us when it points us to the God of all strength. The infinite God who transcends all things has come near to us. He has stooped low through the person of Jesus Christ to meet us in our weakness and fill us with His strength.

We serve a God who has no limits. What comfort for us as limited people! Our circumstances do not limit Him. The laws of science do not limit Him. Our weakness does not limit Him. He works in our simple lives with His infinite power and love. He meets us in our weakness. He is limitless and far beyond our understanding. And though He is far beyond our comprehension, He makes Himself known to us. Though in this life we will never fully understand the infinite nature of who He is, He enters into a relationship with us and reveals Himself to us.

Our response to our infinite God should be like Paul's in Romans 11:33-36. We stand in awe of who He is. We worship. We ascribe to our infinite God the glory that is due to His great name.

Oh, the depth of the riches

both of the wisdom and of the knowledge of God!

How unsearchable his judgments

and untraceable his ways!

For who has known the mind of the Lord?

Or who has been his counselor?

And who has ever given to God,

that he should be repaid?

For from him and through him

and to him are all things.

To him be the glory forever. Amen.

What does it mean that God is infinite? Why is this a good thing?

In what ways are you aware that you do not possess this attribute?

How are you sometimes tempted to live like you are infinite?

WEEK TWO *day three*

"He is *who He is*, and His character *will never change*."

Immutable

Read Psalm 19:14, Psalm 33:11, Psalm 90:2, Psalm 102:26-28, Malachi 3:6, Hebrews 13:8, James 1:17

God is immutable, which is to say that He is unchanging. He is always the same. He is always Himself, always possessing the fullness of all of His attributes. He does not change with the changing world. He is constant, steady, and sure.

Scripture expresses God's immutability by declaring His steadfastness and His unchangeableness. Scripture describes the Lord as our Rock. Perhaps one of the places that we see this attribute most on display is in the book of Exodus when the Lord reveals Himself as the "I AM." He is who He is, and His character will never change. God will always be the same, even as the seasons, culture, and world shift.

The immutability of God should bring us immense comfort because His unchanging nature means that we can trust His Word, which is also unchanging. The truth of Scripture is eternal truth. It does not need to be changed for a changing world. Additionally, God's plans and purposes, as revealed in Scripture, do not change because they flow from His immutable character (Psalm 33:11). What God purposed in Himself before the ages began is still His plan. He will bring His people to Himself and pay the ransom for His own from every tribe, tongue, and nation. We can have confidence in His character, in His Word, and His will.

Hebrews 13:8 also shows us that God's immutable character is perfectly displayed for us in Jesus. He is the same yesterday, today, and forever. We never have to worry about Him changing His mind or losing His love for us. The love for us that He declares in the Scriptures will always remain because His character is unchanging (Ephesians 3:18-19).

As humans, it is hard for us to wrap our minds around these concepts. We are always changing. Our circumstances and life experiences mold us. Our bodies change with every passing year. Our opinions change on everything from our theology to politics to our favorite activities and foods. Our routines change in different seasons, and our latest obsession often falls to the wayside in just a few months. In our vapor-like lives, everything can change in a moment. One phone call can alter the course of our lives. We are not immutable.

In fact, we are made to change. As believers in Christ, we are made to grow in sanctification. We are designed to grow in grace and relationship with our Savior, little by little. We are called to turn from our sin and change through the power of the Spirit.

But sometimes, we grasp at this attribute that is reserved for God alone. We do not want things to change, and we are convinced that we are the way we are, and nothing will ever change that. We crave the unchanging, but sadly we often look to other people, things, or circumstances to fulfill this craving. We look to our spouse to be a rock for us that only God can be. We dread the thought of friendships growing apart. We do not even like to change the simplest parts of our routines. We crave the eternal and the immutable, but by doing this, we make idols out of earthly things.

Yet, we know all too well the changes in life. We see spouses grow apart, and children stop speaking to the parents who raised them. We have seen friendships fall apart, and the lives of people crumble from one phone call or one diagnosis. We understand that people have days when they are not feeling themselves, and we have felt it ourselves. But this is not our God. He does not change. He is always the same—always constant. He never has a day when He is not Himself. And because of His unchanging character, our relationship with Him is altogether different than any other relationship we will ever have. There is an untold number of things that we set up as idols in our hearts, and we yearn for them to fulfill the longing in our souls. But there is only one who ever will, and that is our immutable and unchangeable God. He is a rock when everything around us is shifting and shaking (Psalm 18:2). He is our God. He is our immutable refuge.

The immutability of God should bring us immense comfort because His unchanging nature means that we can trust His Word, which is also unchanging.

How do you find comfort in the immutability of God?

What things have changed in your life in the past year?
How does God's immutability help you to face changes?

To what people or things do you look to bring contentment and satisfaction that only God can give?

day three QUESTIONS

WEEK TWO *day four*

"
The *uncreated* One *created* all things.
"

Self-Existent

Read Psalm 90:1-2, Acts 17:28, John 1:1-4, John 5:26

God is completely self-existent. He was not created but exists by His power alone. There was never a moment when God did not exist. The attribute of God's self-existence is one that surpasses our understanding. With created and finite minds, we try to understand a self-existent and infinite God.

Look around at the world that was created. A self-existent God created every person, every animal, every mountain, every flower, and every tree. The uncreated One created all things. We speak of humans as creative, but we do not wholly understand what it truly means to create. Only God can bring something from nothing.

God is completely different from us. We are needy. We grow weary. We feel lonely. But God does not. And because He is fully self-sufficient, He alone has the ability to fulfill the desires of our hearts. He has the power to meet our needs (Philippians 4:19). He has the power to sustain our lives and fill our lungs with breath (Acts 17:28). He is our Creator and our Sustainer, and without Him, we would not exist.

A.W. Tozer said, "All our problems and their solutions are theological." Let those words soak into your hearts. Tozer was in no way denying that we need things like medicine, clothing, shelter, and food. But when we step back, we can see that all solutions are rooted in God because all things are rooted in God. Without Him, there would be nothing. The gifts of common grace like medicine for disease and sickness, rain for crops, and food on the table are gifts that flow from a loving Father to all of His creation, regardless of whether they acknowledge God or not. All things flow from Him, and all things are made to glorify Him.

We often try to live as though we can control the outcomes in our lives. We grasp for success, thinking that we can achieve it on our own, but all things flow from Him, and the good that we have is a gift of His grace. We think of ourselves as "self-made" when we were made by His gracious hand. We look for created things to fill the aching void of our hearts, but they have no power to satisfy us. As Romans 1:26-32 explains, idolatry happens when we worship created things instead of the Creator. Somehow our sin has sold us on the lie that we should crave the gifts instead of the Lord, our giver.

Yet, our self-existent God does not leave us grasping for empty things that will never satisfy us. The gospel—the good news of Jesus's death and resurrection—meets us in our need and points us to the only One who satisfies. John 1:1-4 describes for us how self-existence is perfectly seen in the person of Jesus. He was from the beginning. The Son of God has always been, and it is He who created the world and everything in it. It is the Son who upholds and sustains all things. And for those wandering in the darkness of our own pursuits of self-existence, Jesus came to earth and humbled Himself to go to the cross and pay the price for our sin. He bore upon Himself the weight of our sin and the punishment for our idolatrous hearts.

The gospel frees us from living as though we are self-existent and reminds us that we were made by the Creator. The gospel connects us to live in an intimate relationship with the only One who will ever fill the void in our hearts. It binds us to a God who has no voids yet fills ours because of His love for His children. All of our problems find their solution in the Lord.

"All our problems and their solutions are theological."

A.W. TOZER

What does God's self-existence teach us about Him?

In what ways are you tempted to live as though you are self-existent?

How does the gospel free us from this thinking?

"It is *in Him* that we find all that we need."

Self-Sufficient

Read Isaiah 40:28-31, Acts 17:24-25, Hebrews 1:1-4, Philippians 4:19

God is self-sufficient. This attribute is closely tied to His self-existence. While the attribute of His self-existence taught us that God was not created and exists independently of all things, this attribute focuses on the fact that God has no needs. He is entirely sufficient and satisfied in Himself. He does not need humanity or the world. He has no need and has never felt the pangs of loneliness. He did not create humanity to fill a void or hole in Himself. He does not grow faint or weary, yet He sustains His weary children through this life (Isaiah 40:28-31).

The hymn, "I Need Thee Every Hour," by Annie Hawk and Robert Lowry, reflects the cry of our hearts to God in every moment, but God has never felt a need for someone like this. He has no needs. And there is no hole in His heart that humanity fills. Before creation, God was perfectly satisfied in Himself, living in perfect unity and community as the triune God (2 Corinthians 13:14 ESV). There is nothing that He depends on, and nothing controls Him (Acts 17:24-25). He is perfect in all of His attributes and sufficient apart from all things.

But this attribute of God is altogether different than us. Humans have needs because we were created with needs. God's self-sufficiency is an incommunicable attribute. It is something that we cannot possess. God designed us to be dependent on many things like food, water, and shelter. And our dependence on all of these things points to our ultimate dependence on God, who is the provider of these things. We were made to be in community with others and need the body of Christ, as displayed in 1 Corinthians 12. We were made to live in dependence on God and others.

Above all, we are made to be sustained by God. It is in Him that we find all that we need. It is Him alone who can satisfy our longing hearts (Psalm 107:9). It is the Lord who fills our lungs with breath and provides our most basic and deepest needs. We need the Lord.

Yet, we tend to want to be self-sufficient like God is. We convince ourselves that we have no needs. We do not want to depend on other people. When others ask us how we are doing, we smile and say "fine," even if our lives are falling apart. We do not want others to know our weaknesses and often do not even admit our deficiencies to ourselves.

Though we may not want to admit it, there are many times that our hearts do not want to depend on the Lord. We do not pray, and we do not open God's Word because we have believed the lie of the world that we are self-sufficient. Though God has given His Word and His Spirit to sustain us, we still try to live in our own strength. These things are rooted in our pride, and our pride tells us that we can do it all in our own strength.

We must look to Jesus. We must look to the gospel. Jesus humbled Himself and became a man. He experienced our weakness and knew every temptation that we would ever face (Luke 4:1-13). He experienced the world's brokenness and felt the pangs of hunger and the parched lips of thirst (Mark 11:12, John 19:28). He went to the cross for us to pay the price for our sins. He who had no need met our needs with Himself. Our neediness points us to the gospel, and it points us to Jesus and what He has done for us. It is a gift to be needy because God will supply our needs (Matthew 5:3-10). He meets every need with Himself.

He is perfect in all of His attributes and sufficient apart from all things.

What does it mean that God is self-sufficient?

In what ways are you tempted to live as though you are self-sufficient?

Why is it a gift to be needy?

day five QUESTIONS

—"I Need Thee Every Hour"—
ANNIE S. HAWK AND ROBERT LOWRY

I need Thee ev'ry hour;
Most gracious Lord
No tender voice like Thine
Can peace afford

I need Thee, oh, I need Thee;
Ev'ry hour I need Thee,
Oh, bless me now, my Savior.
I come to Thee

I need Thee ev'ry hour
Stay Thou nearby
Temptations lose their pow'r
When Thou art nigh.

I need Thee ev'ry hour;
In joy or pain,
Come quickly and abide
Or life is vain.

I need Thee ev'ry hour
Teach Thy will
And Thy rich promises
In me fulfill.

WEEK TWO
Scripture Memory

Lord, there is no one like you.
You are great; your name
is great in power.

—

JEREMIAH 10:6

week two REFLECTION
Review all passages from the week

Summarize the main points from this week's Scripture readings.

What did you observe from this week's passages about God and His character?

What do this week's passages reveal about the condition of mankind and yourself?

How do these passages point to the gospel?

How should you respond to these Scriptures? What specific action steps can you take this week to apply them in your life?

Write a prayer in response to your study of God's Word. Adore God for who He is, confess sins He revealed in your own life, ask Him to empower you to walk in obedience, and pray for anyone who comes to mind as you study.

WEEK THREE *day one*

"*We* are limited, but *God* is not."

Omnipresent

Read Psalm 139:7-10, Jeremiah 23:23-24, Colossians 1:15-20, 1 Kings 8:27

The attribute of God's omnipresence leaves us in awe. Omnipresence means that God can be in all places at once and is something no other person or thing can claim to have. This attribute belongs to God alone. He is everywhere in all of creation, and yet He is near to His children. The God who holds the world together is also Immanuel, God with us. God's omnipresence is far too great for our finite minds to comprehend, and yet it is one of the greatest comforts for us.

The omnipresence of God is an immense gift to the Church. God is present with His people in New York City, and He is present with His people in China. He is just as present in Texas as He is in Pakistan. There is no place outside the scope of His presence (Psalm 139-7-10). He is there. He is here. He is near.

God's omnipresence reminds us that God is altogether different than us. Try as we might, we cannot be in even just two places at once. Yet, the Lord our God is never stretched thin. We are limited, but God is not. Nevertheless, we push hard against our limitations. We want to do it all, and we pack our schedules full as we try to be in more than one place. In some ways, modern technology has given us the illusion of being in more than one place at once. We can Facetime a friend across the world, and we can join a Zoom call from the comfort of our living room. Yet, often in our search for omnipresence, we end up not being fully present anywhere.

God's omnipresence also teaches us that there is no such thing as a secret sin. We may hide our sin from others, but we can never hide it from an all-present God. He sees all that we do in public and in private. He sees not just our actions but also our hearts and our minds. What a sobering realization to understand that there are sins that we commit in the presence of God that we would never commit in the presence of other people. We cannot hide from Him or run from His presence. The great comfort of His presence is also a shining spotlight on our sinfulness and need.

Though God's omnipresence should be sobering to us, it should also be one of the greatest comforts in the life of the child of God. We are never alone (Joshua 1:9). Even when we feel alone, His presence is near. This means that God's presence is not limited to a single location. It means that we do not need to be within the four walls of our church in order to worship, but we can worship in every moment of our lives. It means that we do not need the perfect quiet time with solitude, our journal, and a lit candle to meet with the Lord. He is just as present in carpool lines and hectic workdays as He is in the stillness of our quiet times.

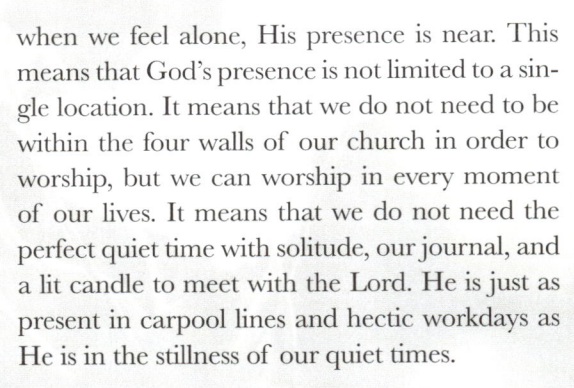

Often the people of God long for the presence of God. This is not a bad thing, but as we study God's omnipresence, it is good for us to understand that God's presence is here. Therefore, what we long for is an awareness of His presence. Stephen Charnock wrote, "God's drawing near to us is not so much His coming to us, but His drawing us to Him." He is present, and now we must ask for Him to make us aware of the truth that we already know. We ask Him to draw us to Himself.

When the pangs of loneliness flood our souls, we can rest in quiet confidence that God is with us. His presence is as real as the tangible things that are before us. We may be tempted to look at the world with its grass, trees, and flowers and imagine that God is somehow not as real as these things. We may be tempted to look at the people we encounter each day and imagine that a conversation with them is more real than time in prayer with God. Yet, how would our walks with God be transformed if we could comprehend the realness of our God? He is greater and deeper and richer than the created things of this world because He is their Creator. Dear child of God, you are never alone.

God is everywhere, but Jesus Christ has made a way for us to uniquely experience God's presence. He who created all things is also Immanuel, God with us (Matthew 1:22-23). Through the incarnation, He drew near to mankind to make us aware of His presence with us. He took on flesh and blood. He walked and ate. He felt the weariness of exhaustion and felt the dust on His feet. He came near to us to show us that God is with us, near us, and for us. He came near to show us that in our need, God does not forsake us, and in our loneliness, we have a refuge. When we were alone in our sin, God drew near and died on a rugged cross in our place (Romans 5:8).

May the omnipresence of God always lift our gaze upward. May it draw us to His side. May it remind us that He is with us, and we are never alone.

> *He is just as present in carpool lines and hectic workdays as He is in the stillness of our quiet times.*

What does God's omnipresence teach us about God?

In what ways are we tempted to live as though we are omnipresent?

How should God's omnipresence change the way that we live?

day one QUESTIONS

WEEK THREE *day two*

> "He knows *all things*, and He knows *us*."

Omniscient

Read Romans 11:33-36, Isaiah 40:27-28, Psalm 139:1-4

God is omniscient. He knows all things. He possesses limitless knowledge of all things because He is the source of all things. He is never caught off guard, and He is never blindsided. And though humans can possess knowledge, the attribute of omniscience is reserved for God alone. Augustine said that "God does not know all creatures…because they exist; they exist because He knows them." Being known by the all-knowing God is at the very essence of who we are as humans.

Our God is never surprised. He is never caught off guard by the events of this world or the circumstances of our lives. This is a gift to God's people. It means that no matter what events shake the world we live in or how blindsided we are in this life, we know God is still in control because He is all-knowing. His sovereign hand is still resting upon us.

We often desire to be omniscient. Perhaps we have never expressed the desire in those words, but it is there nonetheless. We distort the good gift of knowledge in a desire to control our lives and the circumstances around us. We use the minds that God has given us to manipulate our circumstances in an attempt to control both our lives and the lives of others. We want to have "all the facts," and we think that somehow this endless pursuit of knowing all the details will give us the control we desire.

As we pine for absolute knowledge, this attribute of God should open our eyes to the matchless love and grace of our God, who knows everything about us and yet chose to rescue and redeem us. Not many of us could know every struggle and sin in others' lives and still love them completely. Yet, He is profoundly aware of our deepest struggles, our most secret sins, and our greatest fears, and He still pursues us. We have no need to hide from Him, and indeed there is not even the possibility of doing so. We are deeply known and deeply loved, and God's attributes are perfectly synchronized to fulfill our every need.

Furthermore, it should come as no surprise to us that God demonstrates His omniscience in Jesus. It is in Jesus that all the treasures of wisdom and knowledge are found (Colossians 2:3). These treasures are given to Him by God, the Father, and it is through knowing Jesus that we know God (Luke 10:21-22). The Son of God left heaven to rescue His children, though He knew their every sin and malady. Though He knows all things, His heart is full of grace and compassion for His own. And believers—those who have put their faith in Christ—can take comfort in the knowledge that His omniscience means that He will never forget His promises or His covenants with His people. He will never forsake His own (Hebrews 13:5).

The omniscience of God is a soothing balm for our anxious souls. He knows all things, and He knows us. He knows every thought of our hearts, every sorrow, and every tear we shed. Our God has drawn near to us through the person of Jesus and His sacrificial work on the cross. We do not have to live in fear. We do not have to replay all of our what-ifs in our minds over and over again. We are loved by a God who already knows what is ahead and is sovereignly in control of it all. We can rest our hearts in Him.

As we pine for absolute knowledge, this attribute of God should open our eyes to the matchless love and grace of our God, who knows everything about us and yet chose to rescue and redeem us.

What does God's omniscience teach you about who He is?

In what ways are you tempted to live as if you are all-knowing?

How does God's infinite knowledge comfort you?

WEEK THREE *day three*

"He created all things by *His Word*."

Omnipotent

Read Psalm 33:8-9, Psalm 147:5, Job 26:14, Jeremiah 32:17, Luke 1:37, Ephesians 3:16-21

God is omnipotent. He holds all power, and His power is limitless. He created all things by His Word. His power not only created but also sustains all of creation. Nothing has been created apart from Him, and every molecule on earth is known and sustained by His power. His sustaining power never ceases. He does not need a break, and as Isaiah reminds us, He does not faint or grow weary (Isaiah 40:28). His limitless power is always used for good and never used for evil, and in this, He is completely distinct from us.

Throughout Scripture, we hear the repeated refrain: Nothing is too difficult for God (Genesis 18:14, Jeremiah 32:17, 27, Luke 18:27). Sometimes it is seen as a longing question, such as in the biblical story of Sarah and her long battle with infertility (Genesis 18:14). Sometimes it is seen in God's miraculous works when God's people stand against seemingly impossible circumstances (Exodus 14, Joshua 6, 2 Kings 6:16-17). Sometimes it comes as a confident assurance, like when the angel spoke to Mary about the promised Son inside her virgin womb (Luke 1:37). The Bible speaks of the supernatural only because God is omnipotent. He holds all power and can do what He pleases. There is no circumstance too difficult, no suffering too deep, and no sinner too lost that He cannot redeem (Ephesians 3:18-21).

We are not strangers to power, though we do not have the limitless power that God holds. We grasp for power and leverage it for personal gain at the expense of other people made in God's image. We naturally look up to those who have power and disregard those who do not. This is tragic evidence of our fallen state.

People often misuse various kinds of power, and in many ways, so many of our world's problems are rooted in an unrestrained desire for power. Some have physical power. They are stronger than others. This power can be used to help the weak or to instill fear. Some have power due to their position or status. They can use their position to minister and serve others or use it to serve themselves. Some have financial power. The wealthy can use their wealth to bless others or to look out only for themselves. There is power in charisma. Some can convince others to do just about anything with their persuasive words and captivating presence. Finally, some have spiritual power, which is vested in spiritual leaders. This power can be used to minister and proclaim the good news of the gospel, or it can be used to manipulate and abuse. When we abuse the power entrusted to us, we defame God's name for selfish gain. When we use our power to serve, we reflect the image of the God who created us (John 13:1-17).

It is essential that we look to Jesus to see how humanity should think of power. He is our perfect example. He did not seek His own position or recognition. He humbled Himself to come to earth to redeem, though He held the whole world in His hands. He did not leverage His power to hurt others, though all power was within Him. Instead, He used His power to heal the sick, the lame, and the blind (Mark 2:17). Most of all, He used His power to make us sons and daughters of God by humbling Himself and going to the cross in our place. He laid down His power to flee from the cross so that His power would live in us (Matthew 27:42). Not even death is a match for His matchless power (2 Timothy 1:10).

The omnipotence of God reminds us that nothing is out of our God's control. Yet, He is also good, loving, and personal. He never uses His power for evil but always uses it for good. There is no prayer that He cannot answer, no suffering too great that He cannot work it for our good, and no sin too ingrained in us that He cannot destroy (Romans 8:28). As the people of God, we are filled with the power of Christ because He is in us. The power that resurrected our dead hearts now enables us to fight our sin and walk by faith. His sovereign power upholds us, and now we can live in light of His power and goodness (1 John 1:7).

It is essential that we look to Jesus to see how humanity should think of power. He is our perfect example.

What does God's omnipotence teach you about who God is?

Is there something that you worry about that God could not fix or redeem? How does God's omnipotence bring you comfort?

What do your worries reveal about your view of God's omnipotence?

day three QUESTIONS

WEEK THREE *day four*

"The *Word of God* reveals to us the *God of the Word.*"

Incomprehensible and Transcendent

Read Psalm 145:3, Isaiah 40:12-18, Isaiah 46:9-11, Isaiah 55:8-9, Romans 11:33-36

God is incomprehensible. He is far beyond our human understanding and unable to be fully known. This entire study aims to know God more, and the study of God's attributes is a worthwhile pursuit. Yet, we need to recognize that we will never exhaust our study of who He is or fully grasp His limitless being. Despite this, as believers, we should dedicate our lives to knowing Him more each moment because through knowing God, we are transformed and able to discern God's will (Romans 12:2).

God is incomprehensible and unable to be fully known, and He is also transcendent, meaning that man cannot grasp His nature. Though this truth may be a little frustrating for a Bible teacher trying to put the majesty of God into words, it also speaks of just how majestic and glorious He is. We can grasp for illustrations to describe who He is, but nothing compares to our God. Thomas Aquinas once said, "God exists infinitely and nothing finite can grasp Him infinitely." Try as we might, we will never be able to fully know or explain the glory of our God.

Our God is incomprehensible, yet He is also knowable. He is transcendent, yet He is also personal. These twin truths show the greatness of who God is. Though we will never wholly comprehend who He is, He invites us to know Him through His Word. Though we will never grasp His transcendent majesty, He also walks with us and knows us intimately.

What does God want us to know about Him? Though we will never exhaust the knowledge of who He is, Scripture teaches us that God desires for us to know Him. The answer to the question of what God wants us to know about Him is found in His Word. It is there that He has revealed Himself to His people. By studying the character of God through His Word, we begin to understand the person of God. The Bible reveals God to us through the unfolding narrative of redemption. Through it, we see how God works in the world, how He interacts with humanity, and how His sovereign plan of redemption was set in place before the world was even created. The Word of God reveals to us the God of the Word.

It is in Jesus, the Word made flesh, that God is most fully revealed to us. It is in Jesus that we see a glimpse of the glory of God (John 1:14). It is Jesus who is our mediator and the one who brings us to God (1 Timothy 2:5). It is Jesus who has come to bridge the impassable gap between sinful humanity and a holy and righteous God (John 14:6). Though we will never completely comprehend God's greatness and glory, we must look to Jesus as God in the flesh who helps our finite hearts understand more of who God is.

Though He is incomprehensible and transcendent, God longs for us to know Him more. As we discussed earlier this week, God knows our every thought and every secret we try to hide. Yet, He came in Jesus to redeem us to Himself. We cannot fully understand Him in our limited state, and we cannot fully understand our hearts (Jeremiah 17:9). However, we can stand in awe that He knows everything about us and still loves us the same.

> *"God exists infinitely and nothing finite can grasp Him infinitely."*
>
> THOMAS AQUINAS

What stands out to you about God's incomprehensibility and transcendence?

How does this attribute make you thankful for Jesus?

How does this attribute push you to Scripture?

day four QUESTIONS

WEEK THREE *day five*

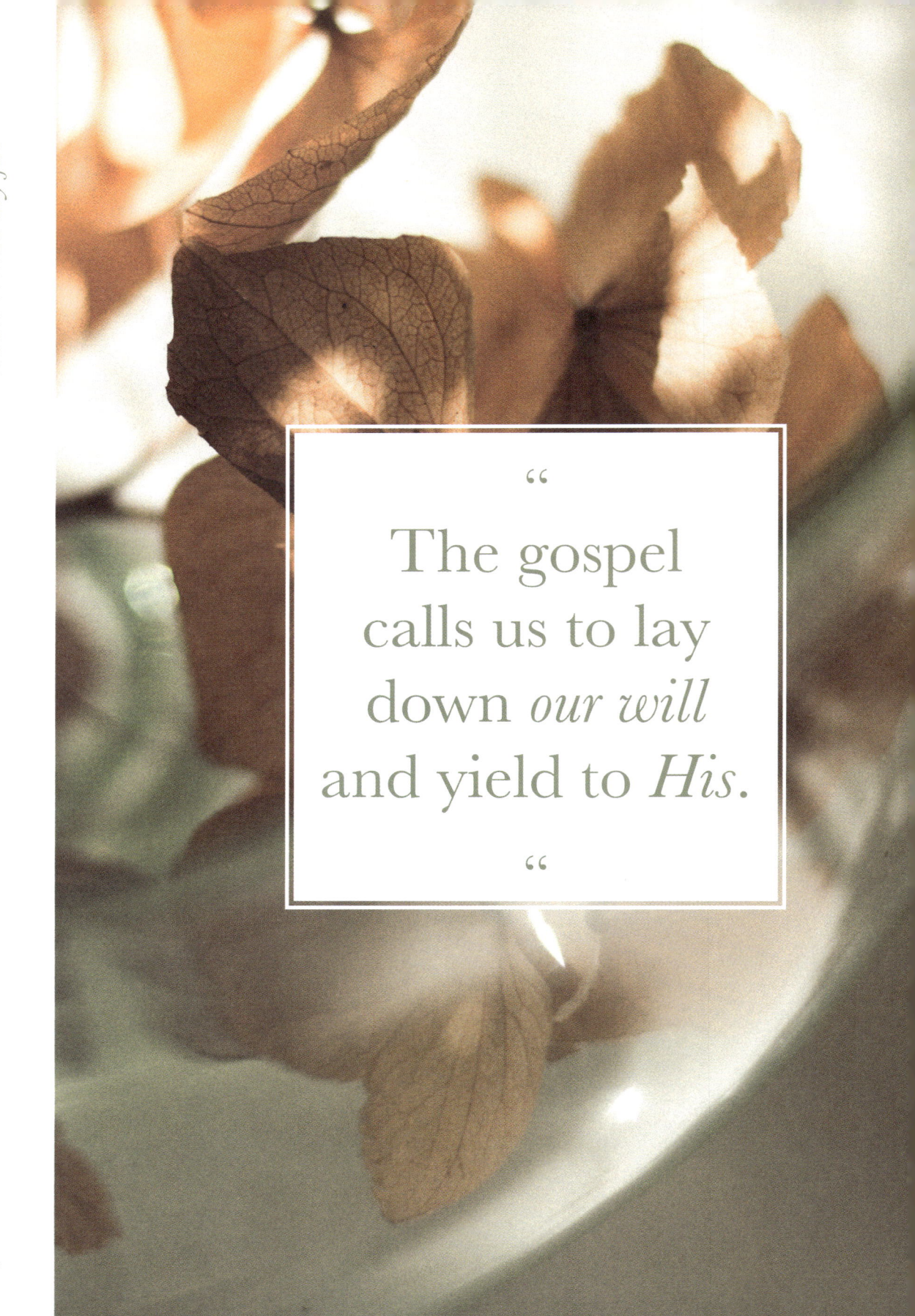

> "The gospel calls us to lay down *our will* and yield to *His*."

Sovereign

Read Job 23:13, Isaiah 14:24, Daniel 4:34-35, Romans 9:14-16, Ephesians 1, Revelation 4:11

God is sovereign. He is in complete control of all things, and He rules over all things. There is nothing that happens in the world outside of His sovereign control. He not only has the power to do all things but also the authority. He is the sovereign King and the Lord of all the earth. He holds all authority in heaven and earth, and everything and everyone bows to His will.

God's sovereignty is often demonstrated in Scripture through the title of "Lord" that is ascribed to God. It describes our God as the Lord of all (1 Corinthians 10:26) and the one in control of all things (Isaiah 45:7). If God were not sovereign, He would not be God. It is difficult for humans to grasp the intricate relationship between God's sovereignty and man's responsibility. Yet, Scripture verifies these truths, and they are in no way in conflict with one another. The words of Romans 9:14-16 echo the declaration that God will have mercy on whom He will have mercy. His sovereign plan will stand, and humanity is responsible for their choices. His sovereignty is a mystery that should bring us to worship.

But God's sovereignty is not impersonal and far off. In fact, God set a plan in motion before the foundations of the world to restore His people to Himself through the person and work of Jesus (1 Peter 1:20).

Jesus's death on the cross was the sovereign plan of God (Acts 2:22-23) so that He could realize His will to dwell with His people. The same God who set His presence in the tabernacle and temple and spoke words of gospel hope through the prophets in the Old Testament is the one who came in the person of Jesus to be Immanuel, God with us (Matthew 1:23). The sovereign Word became flesh and came to dwell among us and in us (John 1:14). Even now, God's Spirit dwells in His people who are His temple (1 Corinthians 3:16). And someday, the people of God will live in His presence forever (Revelation 21).

We are not sovereign. Sovereignty is an incommunicable attribute of God. Yet, as discussed on day two of this week, we still grasp for control. Our will is not certain, yet our hearts demand that our will be done. We want to be sovereign over our lives. We want to be lord of all that we do. We want authority and control. We want to do what we want to do, and we want to do it our way. But the gospel of Jesus Christ calls us to another way. The gospel calls us to lay down our will and yield to His. Our God calls us to pray for His will to be done on earth as it is in heaven (Matthew 6:10). The sovereignty of God calls us to daily submission and daily dependence.

God's sovereignty is our comfort when life does not go the way we planned or expected. When our wills are shattered, we begin to see that His will is always best, even when it is hard, even when it hurts, even when it involves suffering and refining. The sovereignty of God teaches us to trust Him.

When we are overwhelmed by life that seems so out of our control, we can rest in His sovereignty. When we are anxious that we may have stepped out of His will, we can know that nothing will deter His will. He is sovereign. That is who He was, who He will be, and who He is. God's sovereignty is difficult for us to grasp because it is so different from who we are as humans, and yet it is the comfort in which we can rest. Our God is sovereign. He is in control. And we are loved by Him.

God's sovereignty is our comfort when life does not go the way we planned or expected.

How are you comforted by God's sovereignty?

In what ways do you grasp for control and try to live as though you are sovereign over your own life?

In what area of your life do you need to be reminded of God's sovereignty?

day five QUESTIONS

WEEK THREE
Scripture Memory

The Lord passed in front of him and proclaimed: The Lord—the Lord is a compassionate and gracious God, slow to anger and abounding in faithful love and truth

—

EXODUS 34:6

week three REFLECTION
Review all passages from the week

Summarize the main points from this week's Scripture readings.

What did you observe from this week's passages about God and His character?

What do this week's passages reveal about the condition of mankind and yourself?

How do these passages point to the gospel?

How should you respond to these Scriptures? What specific action steps can you take this week to apply them in your life?

Write a prayer in response to your study of God's Word. Adore God for who He is, confess sins He revealed in your own life, ask Him to empower you to walk in obedience, and pray for anyone who comes to mind as you study.

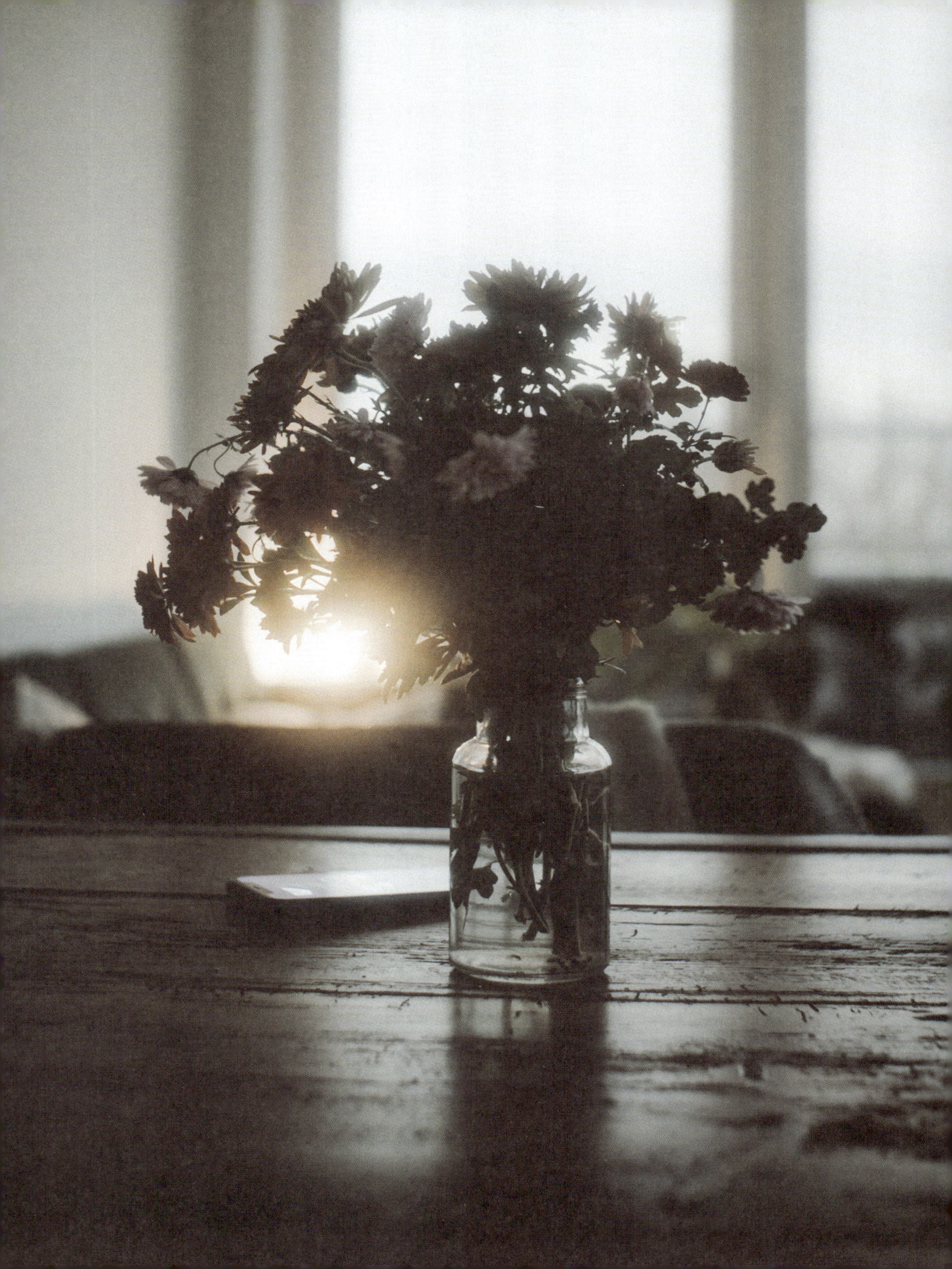

Communicable Attributes

We are going to spend the last part of this study exploring God's communicable attributes. These are the attributes that we can possess. While it is important to note that all of these attributes are God-given and present themselves as we grow in our relationship with Him, there are some that we are more naturally inclined to possess.

Take a moment to review the list of communicable attributes. Are there some that are easier for you to reflect in your life? Which ones are more difficult for you to live out each day? Remembering that we are not transformed due to our effort but by the Holy Spirit living in us, pray that as you continue this study, God will grow you in your ability to reflect all of His attributes.

Holy	*Merciful*
Loving	*Gracious*
Good	*Jealous*
Truthful	*Patient*
Just	*Wise*
Wrathful	*Faithful*

WEEK FOUR *day one*

"
In Christ,
we see the
exact imprint
of *the holiness
of God.*
"

Holy

Read Exodus 15:11, Leviticus 19:2, Isaiah 6:3, Psalm 29:1-2, Ephesians 1:4-6, Revelation 4:8

God is holy. He is sacred, set apart, pure, and undefiled. This attribute proclaims the very nature of God. God is holy in all that He is and all that He does. This attribute also, like some other characteristics, influences all of His other attributes. His love is a holy love. His wrath is a holy wrath. And His justice is a holy justice. Holiness is who God is.

This attribute is particularly significant because it is the attribute that is most often used to describe God and the attribute most often linked with the name of God. Appearing more than 600 times throughout Scripture, the word "holy" stands out as something we should pay attention to. Over and over throughout Scripture, there is a recognition of God's holiness and the holiness of His name. And throughout Scripture, we see the name of God used to describe who God is. The holiness of God and His name is foundational to the character of God. Even in the Lord's prayer, we see Jesus teach the disciples to pray for God's name to be holy or hallowed (Matthew 6:9). And in Revelation 4:8, there is a scene in heaven in which day and night God is declared to be holy, holy, holy. It is the only attribute that is listed three times in a row as a description of God. The holiness of God points us to the essence of who our triune God is. Indeed He is holy, holy, holy.

The holiness of God sets God apart from all other things. He is distinct from all of creation. All that He does and all that He is is pure. He is unstained and undefiled. There is nothing that pollutes His perfection. There is no limit to His holiness. The holiness of God humbles us because of how dissimilar He is from us. Words seem to fail us as we seek to describe the holiness of God because of how distinct God's holiness is. Holiness is the essence of the person of God.

As we meditate on God's holiness, we must look to Jesus. In Christ, we see the exact imprint of the holiness of God (Hebrews 1:3). Christ is our example, and He is our mediator. In His life and death, Jesus was perfectly holy. It is at the cross that we see the holiness of God on display. It is there that a God so perfect in holiness and utterly incapable of ignoring sin watched on as the Son of God bore the weight of the sin of God's people. It is there that God displayed

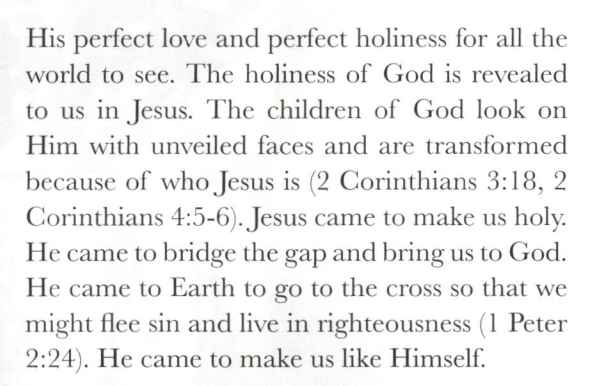

His perfect love and perfect holiness for all the world to see. The holiness of God is revealed to us in Jesus. The children of God look on Him with unveiled faces and are transformed because of who Jesus is (2 Corinthians 3:18, 2 Corinthians 4:5-6). Jesus came to make us holy. He came to bridge the gap and bring us to God. He came to Earth to go to the cross so that we might flee sin and live in righteousness (1 Peter 2:24). He came to make us like Himself.

In this attribute, we see a shift from the incommunicable attributes that we have discussed up until this point. This attribute, which is perfectly displayed in God, is one that He calls us to embody as well. In this and the following communicable attributes, we will see how we were designed to reflect God's image.

"Be holy, because I am holy" is the call of God to His own (1 Peter 1:16). Through the power of the gospel, the children of God are made positionally holy, which means that we are declared holy the moment that we trust Christ as our Savior. Through union with Christ, we are declared to be righteous and set apart as holy people. That is to say: God calls us to be who He has declared us to be. It is also worth noting that while we are positionally holy, God is making us more and more holy throughout our lives. This work is called sanctification, and it is a lifelong process for every child of God. It is the process of God making us like Himself, which is evident in the growth of the fruit of the Spirit in us (Galatians 5:22-23). So we stand in awe of God's holiness, and we stand in awe of the fact that He is transforming us moment by moment into a person who reflects the image of a holy God.

God calls us to be who He has declared us to be.

day one QUESTIONS

How do you define God's holiness?

What does God's holiness teach you about who He is and who you are?

In what practical ways can you grow in holiness?

WEEK FOUR *day two*

"*Nothing* can separate us from God's love."

Loving

Read Exodus 34:6-7, Psalm 136, Isaiah 54:10, John 3:16, Romans 5:1-8, Galatians 2:20

God is loving. God is eternally, enduringly, steadfastly loving, and affectionate. He does not forsake or betray His covenant love. The Bible is the story about God and His love for His own. The love of God is central to His essence. And there is perhaps no more comforting truth in all of Scripture than the message of God's love. "Jesus loves me this I know / For the Bible tells me so" is more than a children's Sunday school song; it is the message of Scripture to a world in need of the love that only God can give.

Moreover, God's love was not born with the creation of the world. It existed long before. Love was present in the Trinity for all of eternity between the Father, Son, and Spirit. Ephesians 1:3-6 tells us that before the foundations of the world, God chose us and set His love on us. Perhaps you have heard it said that love is a choice. This is true, and Scripture tells us that God has chosen to love His children. God loved us at our darkest, and He pursued us and brought us into His light. The flood of God's love pours over His people, and the streams of His mercy never cease.

It is important to note that the love of God is not in opposition to His other attributes. He is loving and also just. He is loving and also holy. He is loving and also wrathful. We must not focus on one attribute while ignoring the other characteristics of our God. While it would be impossible to over-emphasize the majesty of God's love, we must seek to know and understand the fullness of God's character in all of His beauty.

We can begin to understand God's love by studying Scripture. In fact, we see the steadfast love of God throughout all of Scripture. Love is the cornerstone of the Bible's story. Through love, God creates covenants in the Old Testament, and in the New Testament, love propels Him to send His only Son to die on the cross for our sins (John 3:16). In Exodus 34, Moses is given a glimpse of God's glory, and included in the Lord's description of Himself is that He abounds in faithful, or steadfast, love. This steadfast love is the *hesed* love of God. This Hebrew word depicts this steadfast, faithful, eternal, covenant-keeping love of God. The English language does not have a single word that can fully encapsulate all that is implied by this beautiful word. This is how God describes Himself. And it is this steadfast love of God that is seen throughout Scripture. It is seen in His patience with His people though they rebel and turn to idols. It is seen in His mercy. It is seen in His grace. And finally, it is seen in Jesus.

God's love is displayed for us in the person of Jesus. It is in Jesus that we understand the depths of God's steadfast love for His people. John 3:16 states the simple declaration that God so loved the world that He gave His Son to die for our sins. The love of God is made visible in Jesus. The "love of God" is more than a trite phrase; the love of God is the gospel. Romans 5:1-8 presents in vivid detail this glorious love. The passage states that this love has been poured out to us by His Spirit. The love of Christ is seen through His incarnation—that God Himself became a human to redeem us back to God. God's love is demonstrated to us in that Jesus died for us while we were still sinners. Jesus has loved us and given Himself for us (Galatians 2:20). This is a personal love from the Son of God to His own.

As the people of God, we are created in His image. We were made to reflect His love to the world around us. We were made to love God and to love others (Matthew 22:35-40). And 1 John 4:19 tells us that the reason we love is that He first loved us. We are to be reflections of the heart of God in this world. If we are struggling to love those around us, we must remember the love of God that has ransomed our wayward souls. Loving God changes the way that we live. The Word of God stirs our hearts to love Him more each day as we learn more and more of who He is.

Nothing can separate us from God's love. That is a promise (Romans 8:38-39). And if there is ever a moment when we find ourselves uncertain of or questioning the love of God for us, let us look to the cross and see God's love displayed there for us through Jesus. To see the love of God, we must turn our eyes upon Jesus. The love of God pursues us, welcomes us, sanctifies us, convicts us, frees us, and brings us to Himself.

We are to be reflections of the heart of God in this world.

How do you describe the love of God?

How has God's love changed your life?

How should God's love for you change how you live in relation to God and other people?

day two QUESTIONS

WEEK FOUR *day three*

"He is good.
He is *always*
good."

Good

Read Psalm 25:8-9, Psalm 34:8, Psalm 100:5, Psalm 107, Psalm 119:68, Nahum 1:7

God is good. He is pure and undefiled. He is kind, and He is flawless. He is safe and secure. He satisfies the longing soul. He is good, and all that He does is good. He is always good. This truth never changes. And there is no aspect of His being or in any of His works that are not utter goodness.

You do not have to read far in Scripture before encountering the goodness of God. The first chapter of Genesis introduces us to a good God from whom flows good things. The creation was good, but it was good only because it reflected the God who had made it. In goodness and grace, He fashioned the world and set in motion His eternal decree. The goodness of God is on display throughout the entire Bible. His goodness is in the creation in Genesis, and it is in the new creation in Revelation's final chapters. The Bible is a testament to a good God who sets in motion His good plan. The Bible is the story of the gospel, and it should come as no surprise to us that the word "gospel" literally means "good news."

The Scriptures declare for us the goodness of God, and so does the world in which we live. Through common grace, God's goodness is displayed to all people. God's lavish kindness is displayed through every good and perfect gift that He has bestowed upon the world. We see His goodness in the beauty of nature and the awe of the rising and setting sun. We experience His goodness as we taste food and wine, as we enjoy the communion of sex, or as we feel the warmth of the sun on a Summer day. The world around us points to God's goodness and kindness and to so many things that He did not have to give us, but He did.

Goodness is who God is; it is His essence. Because it is who He is, there is nothing in Him that is not good. Even His wrath and justice are good. The book of Romans calls us to behold the goodness and severity of God (Romans 11:22). Though from our human understanding, these traits may seem in opposition, they are perfectly harmonized in the person of God. Even His wrath is good. And the people of God can rest secure in His goodness.

His goodness is also infinite and abundant. Like an ever-flowing stream, the goodness of God flows from our God to His people. Repeated throughout the Psalms is the call, "Give thanks to the Lord, for He is good" (Psalm 106:1, 107:1, 118:1, 29, 136:1). These words often open psalms of praise, encouraging us to worship the Lord for His goodness to His people. Passages like Psalm 107 also provide for us an exposition of the goodness of God. These verses state His goodness and then describe how that goodness is demonstrated toward His children.

In Luke 2, angels appeared to shepherds announcing the birth of Jesus the Messiah. Scripture tells us that they came to proclaim the good news. The word used here for "good news" is the Greek *euangelizō*, and it is the word that is most often translated as "gospel." This is important to note because the story of Scripture is the story of the good news of the gospel, which is centered on Jesus Christ. And the goodness of God is most fully displayed for us in Jesus.

Jesus is perfectly good. He is the goodness of God in human flesh. And Jesus bore the wrath of God for us so that we may experience the goodness and kindness of God toward us. We look to Jesus, and we see the goodness of God.

Goodness is a way in which we are called to be like God. We are called to be good. The goodness of God is something that we should celebrate and emulate. God's goodness should lead us to gratitude and worship. And His goodness should also lead us to repentance (Romans 2:4). Our life should be one of tasting and seeing His goodness in every moment. Even the simple act of participating in communion gives us a chance to taste, see, and remember His goodness to us. And the goodness of God should compel us to do and be good because He has made us into goodness through the imputed righteousness of His Son. If you are unfamiliar with imputed righteousness, it is the idea that we are declared holy by God through faith in Jesus. Therefore, God calls us "good" because Christ is good, and our lives are a process of sanctification and becoming who He has already declared us to be.

Finally, His goodness flows to His people and assures us of His kindness and love. His goodness provides security when we do not understand His plan (Romans 8:28). When we are discouraged by our sin yet again, we cling to the goodness of God, who is fashioning us into His image day by day. We can press on and not grow weary and tired of doing good because He is at work. When others are bad and harmful to us, we rest secure in the goodness of God, who is always good. He is good. He is always good.

Our life should be one of tasting and seeing His goodness in every moment of life.

How would you describe the goodness of God?

How has your life evidenced God's goodness in ways both big and small?

How is God calling you to reflect His goodness?

day three QUESTIONS

WEEK FOUR *day four*

"God *is* true,
and all that He
does is true."

Truthful

Read Numbers 23:19, Psalm 119:160, Isaiah 45:19, John 1:14, John 14:6, Romans 1:25, Hebrews 6:18-19, 1 John 5:20

God is truth. God is our measurement of what is true and factual, and it is by Him that we can discern truth and falsehood. God is the standard for truth in the world, and His Word is fully true and trustworthy. God cannot lie, and He always keeps His Word.

What is truth? Truth is the actual state of things. It is fact. It is authentic and accurate. God is truth and the measurement for all that is true. The Word of God and the God of the Word are our standards for truth.

The story of the Bible begins with the God of truth making a good creation, but by the third chapter of Genesis, God's truth was already twisted. From the deceitful comments of the evil serpent in the garden of Eden to the rationalization of sin by Adam, the battle between good and evil has always been a battle between the truth of God and the lies of the enemy. It is no wonder that Paul in the book of Romans described the unrighteous as those who had exchanged God's truth for the lies of the world (Romans 1:25). The lies of the enemy and the sin in our hearts have caused humanity to run from the God of truth to the lies of the world.

But God is altogether different from fallen humanity. God is true, and all that He does is true. His Word is true, and He always keeps His promises. He does not deceive, and His words are never a trick. We can trust Him. Though all that God says is true, God's truth is more than the things God says. Truth is who God is. He is the definition of truth, and all truth is defined by who He is.

Our world can struggle with absolute truth, which is the concept that ideas are true regardless of the context, belief system, or place in time. To some, this concept seems rigid and boring. Much of our modern culture embraces the idea of moral relativism, where each person determines individual truth. This is a scary concept when we reflect on Scripture that tells us that the hearts of men are deceitful and wicked and that the ways of man are the ways of death (Jeremiah 17:9, Proverbs 14:12). You may have heard people speak of following "their truth," yet this so-called truth is foreign to the Word of God. Only God can establish truth, and all truth is His truth.

The truthfulness of God points us to the gospel. It reminds us that our God is a covenant-keeping God; He keeps His promises. This should guard our hearts against being cynical and cause us to live in the hope that the gospel of God pours out for us. The truthfulness of God is manifested and embodied in the person of Jesus Christ. He is the way, the truth, and the life (John 14:6). He is full of grace and truth. In looking to Jesus, we can see what is true and understand God's truth lived out in the world.

God is true, and He calls us to be people of truth. However, Scripture points us to specific ways that we are supposed to live out the truth. We are called to speak with truth and grace, just like our Savior exemplifies for us (John 1:14).

We are also called to love and defend the truth with gentleness, just like Jesus did (2 Timothy 2:24-25, 1 Peter 3:15). Our message should not change depending on who is listening. But in all situations, we should overflow with the truth of God's Word and His loving compassion.

The truthfulness and trustworthiness of God are bedrocks of our faith. God cannot lie, and that gives us hope and confidence. God will do what He has promised. His Word is true, and we can cling to it no matter what life may bring. We do not live without hope but live in the truth of the gospel and God's Word.

> *God is our measurement of what is true and factual, and it is by Him that we can discern truth and falsehood.*

How does God being truthful impact your life?

In what ways are you tempted to be untruthful?
How can you imitate God in being truthful?

Why does God's truthfulness give you assurance and hope?

day four QUESTIONS

WEEK FOUR *day five*

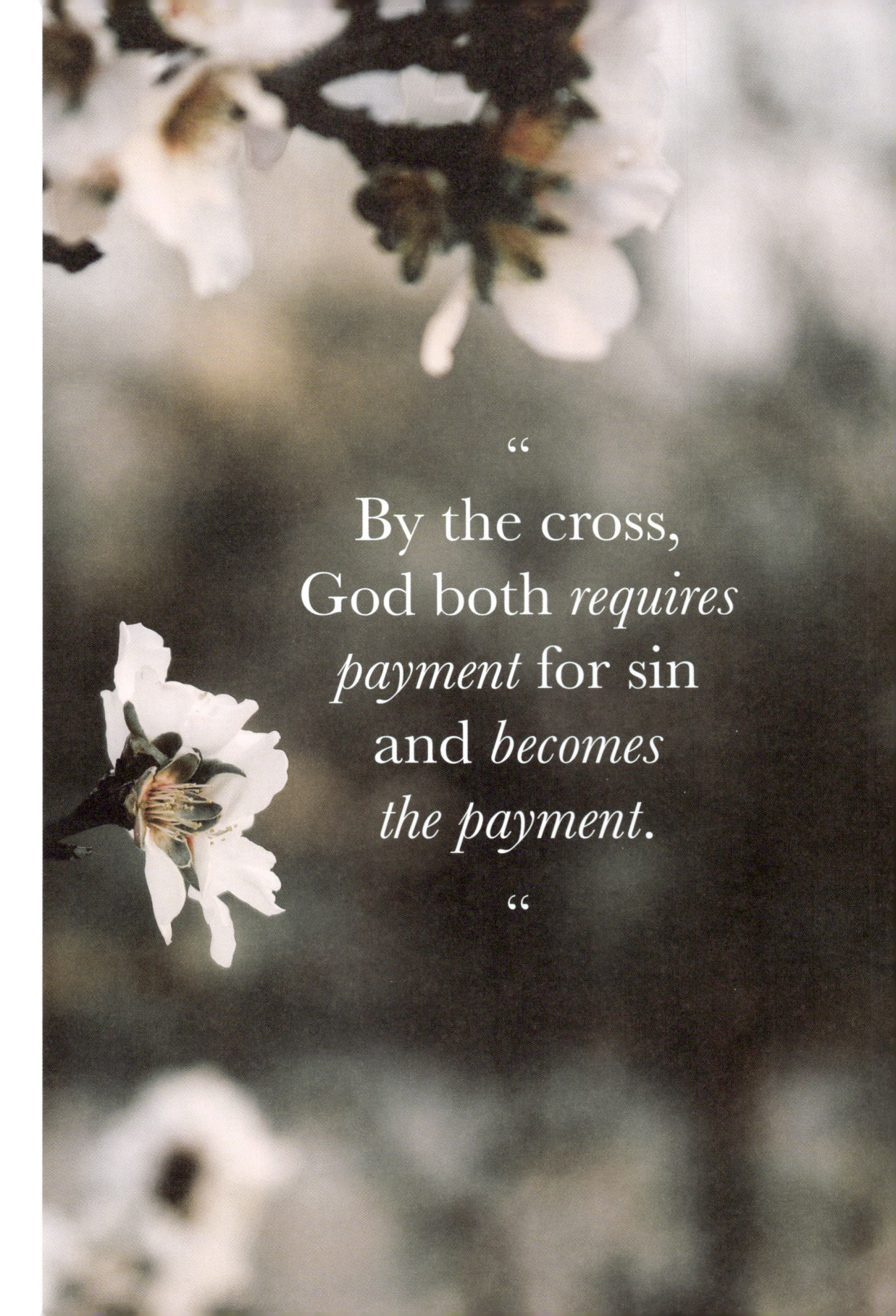

"
By the cross, God both *requires payment* for sin and *becomes the payment.*
"

Just

Read Genesis 18:25, Deuteronomy 32:3-4, Psalm 9:7-8, Psalm 89:14, Micah 6:8, Romans 3:26

God is just. He governs in perfect justice. He acts in accordance with justice. In Him, there is no wrongdoing or dishonesty. He does what is right—always. There is never any corruption in His justice. He determines right from wrong, and His Word declares His just law.

Justice can be hard for us to understand. Even in the church, everyone seems to have their own opinions of what justice is. While some of God's attributes, such as His love, mercy, and grace, seem immediately comforting, it can be hard to understand how God's justice is a comfort to His people.

As a God of justice, God always does what is right. This means that we can trust all that He does. In Genesis 18:25, Abraham is concerned about the righteous dying with the wicked and asks God whether the judge of all the earth will do right. God justly responds that He would spare the righteous from dying. This conversation reminds us of the emphatic truth that He will always do what is right. We can know His answer to Abraham is just because it is consistent with God's character in the rest of Scripture: the righteous will always be spared (Psalm 1:5-6, Proverbs 12:21, Job 36:7, 1 Peter 3:12). From our limited perspective, it can be hard to understand His justice, but the children of God can truly rest in His goodness and justice.

In the world, justice is often skewed. Sometimes even systems of so-called justice oppress and mistreat the most vulnerable. Prejudice and partiality skew the justice systems of the world. But Scripture points us to a God of justice who is altogether different. His justice never oppresses and always does what is right (Proverbs 14:31). He is never prejudiced, and He never shows partiality (Galatians 3:28, James 2:1-13). He is just, and He is good.

Scripture is the place where we must run to know the just ways of God, for it is His Word that teaches us who He is. His Word and His law should be our constant delight. His continuous moral equity should bring us peace in the knowledge that though we do not always understand His ways, we can trust that His justice will endure.

The Old Testament prophets repeatedly speak of the justice of God and the call to the people of God to be people of justice. When they oppressed the neediest, they judged. When they neglected the vulnerable, God demanded justice and care for the oppressed widows and orphans (Exodus 22:22-24). When the nation of Israel did not live justly, God judged them for their evil and oppressive ways (Ezekiel 7).

Finally, if we want to understand the justice of God, we must look to Jesus. Romans 3:26 points us to the truth that God is both the just and the justifier. The justice of God demands that the cross of Christ was necessary to make a just payment for the sin of the people of God. By the cross, God both requires payment for sin and becomes the payment.

As believers, we are called to be just as God is just. Our character should be ever-growing in justice, fairness, righteousness, uprightness, consistency, and impartiality. We should seek justice for the oppressed and live humbly before the Lord our God (Micah 6:8). Justice is a call for all believers because it is who God is. We must never forget that the just payment for our sin was death, yet in His justice, love, and mercy, Jesus took that payment on Himself so that we could be the sons and daughters of God.

As a God of justice, God always does what is right. This means that we can trust all that He does.

How do you find comfort in God's justice?

In what ways are you tempted to be unjust?

Day-to-day, are you just in your treatment of your husband, siblings, children, friends, strangers, etc.? How can you continue to develop this attribute of God in your life?

WEEK FOUR

Scripture Memory

The Lord is great and is highly praised; his greatness is unsearchable.

—

PSALM 145:3

week four REFLECTION
Review all passages from the week

Summarize the main points from this week's Scripture readings.

What did you observe from this week's passages about God and His character?

What do this week's passages reveal about the condition of mankind and yourself?

How do these passages point to the gospel?

How should you respond to these Scriptures? What specific action steps can you take this week to apply them in your life?

Write a prayer in response to your study of God's Word. Adore God for who He is, confess sins He revealed in your own life, ask Him to empower you to walk in obedience, and pray for anyone who comes to mind as you study.

WEEK FIVE *day one*

> "We can *reflect the image of God* by hating sin the way that God does."

Wrathful

Read Psalm 69:24, Psalm 147:11, Nahum 1:2-6, John 3:36, Romans 1:18, Revelation 19:15

Our God is wrathful. In His divine will, He has declared what is good and righteous, and He stands in opposition to all that is evil. He bases His wrath on the foundation of His holiness, righteousness, and justice.

Of all the attributes of God, this one is most often abused. Many ignore God's wrath. They pretend that it does not exist. It does not usually come up in popular Christian books or devotionals, and there are not many sermons on the wrath of God. It is an attribute that many ignore. However, when we ignore this attribute of God, we deprive ourselves of a full understanding of who God is because wrath is part of who God is. We cannot understand many of the other attributes without the knowledge of God's holy wrath.

The opposite can also be true. Though perhaps it does not happen as often as ignoring God's wrath, some place an overemphasis on this attribute in an attempt to elicit fear and implement legalism. These people present God as harsh and bitterly angry. They hold signs that declare the coming judgment with no mention of the grace that has given sinful humanity a way to escape God's wrath.

God's attributes must be seen in accordance with one another. They should not be siloed because they work in harmony with one another. With this in mind, we should understand that we cannot fully understand God without knowledge of His divine wrath.

God's wrath is His fervent determination to punish sin, and the wrath of God declares the heavy weight of our sin. The wrath of God should also encourage us to evangelize and share the gospel with those around us. His wrath creates an urgency to proclaim the gospel to those we love. J.I. Packer said that "God's wrath in the Bible is something which people choose for themselves." This should compel us to share the hope of the gospel and the remedy for the wrath of God.

Jesus was angry without sin, and He stands as an example of how we should have wrath toward evil and desire to glorify God's name amid a sinful world. Jesus's wrath teaches us that wrath in itself is not sin, but often we allow the outworking of our wrath to be evil, or we are filled with anger for selfish reasons.

Jesus's life demonstrates the wrath of God, but it is also in Jesus that we see the holiness of God's wrath against sin (John 2:13-22, Matthew 21:12-13, Matthew 23:1-4, 33). God's wrath for sin is satisfied at the cross. Through Christ's sacrificial death, sinners are brought back to God and escape His holy wrath. In ourselves, we have no way to escape the wrath to come, but through Jesus, we are made holy as He is holy. Jesus bore the wrath of God so that we would not have to.

Now, as believers, we live in the fear of the Lord, knowing that Jesus has satisfied God's wrath in our place. We can reflect the image of God by hating sin the way that God does. Instead of making jokes or laughing about sin, we can seek to understand the devastation that it brings and how it attacks God's name and glory. We can understand who God is more by knowing that He is a God of wrath.

> *Jesus was angry without sin, and He stands as an example of how we should have wrath toward evil and desire to glorify God's name amid a sinful world.*

Why do you think this is an attribute of God that is often skipped? Why have you been tempted not to think about this truth?

Why can we be grateful for God's wrath?

How can we reflect this attribute of God without sinning?

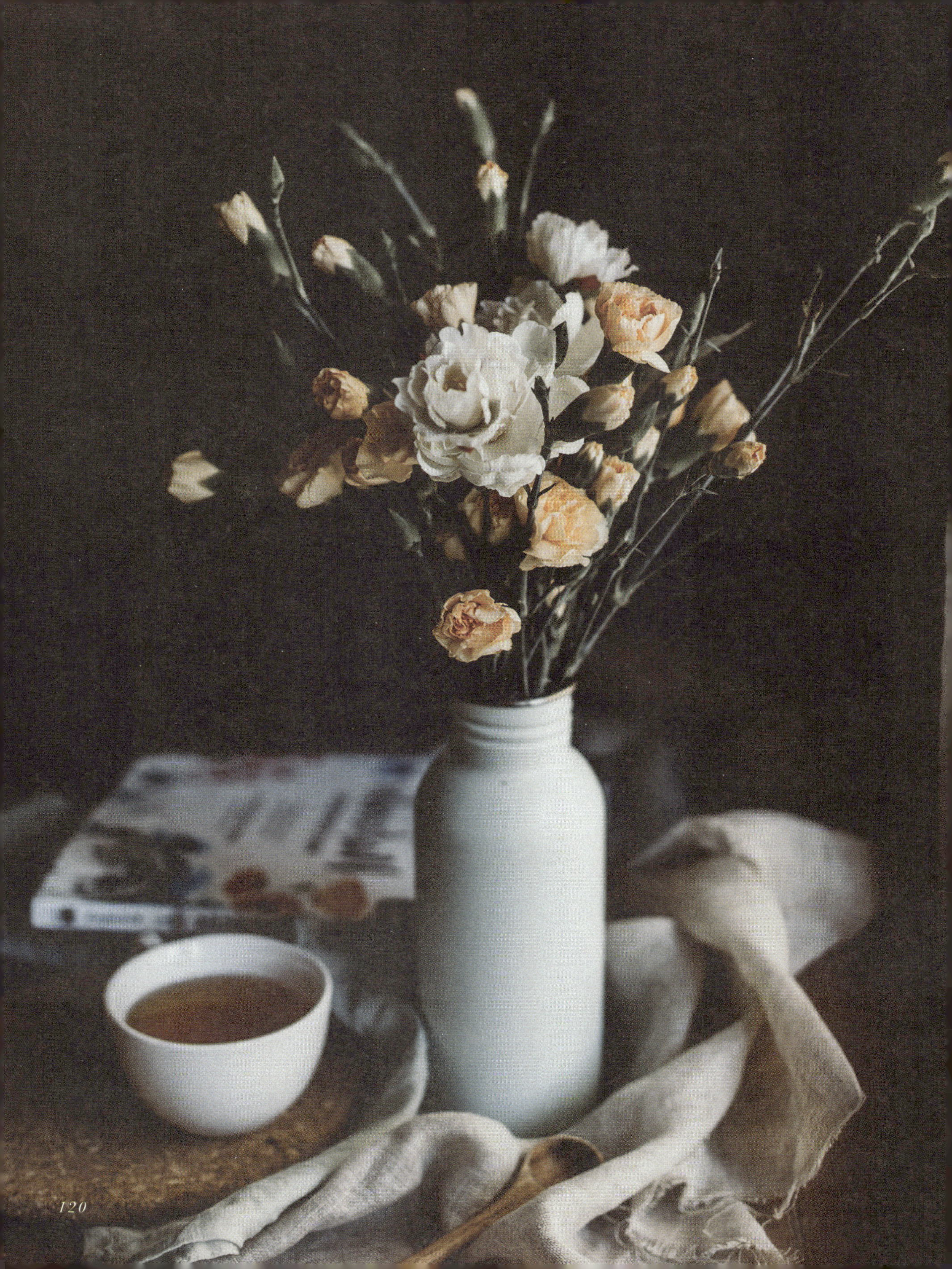

— *Misunderstanding God's Wrath* —

God's wrathful attribute can be complex for some to process because they have never seen righteous anger. Instead, they may have seen someone they trusted use anger to manipulate and abuse them or someone they loved. This is not the wrath of God, but it can still impact the way we interpret God's wrath.

If this is a part of your story, we would first like to say that we are so sorry that you or someone you love has been poorly treated. Second, we encourage you to remember that the injustice against you or your loved ones is exactly where God's righteous wrath is placed—not on the victim but on those who harm others. Third, take a few minutes to reflect on and pray about how the anger of other people has affected your view of God.

You may need to take additional steps like talking to a trusted family member, friend, or counselor to further process your experiences.

WEEK FIVE *day two*

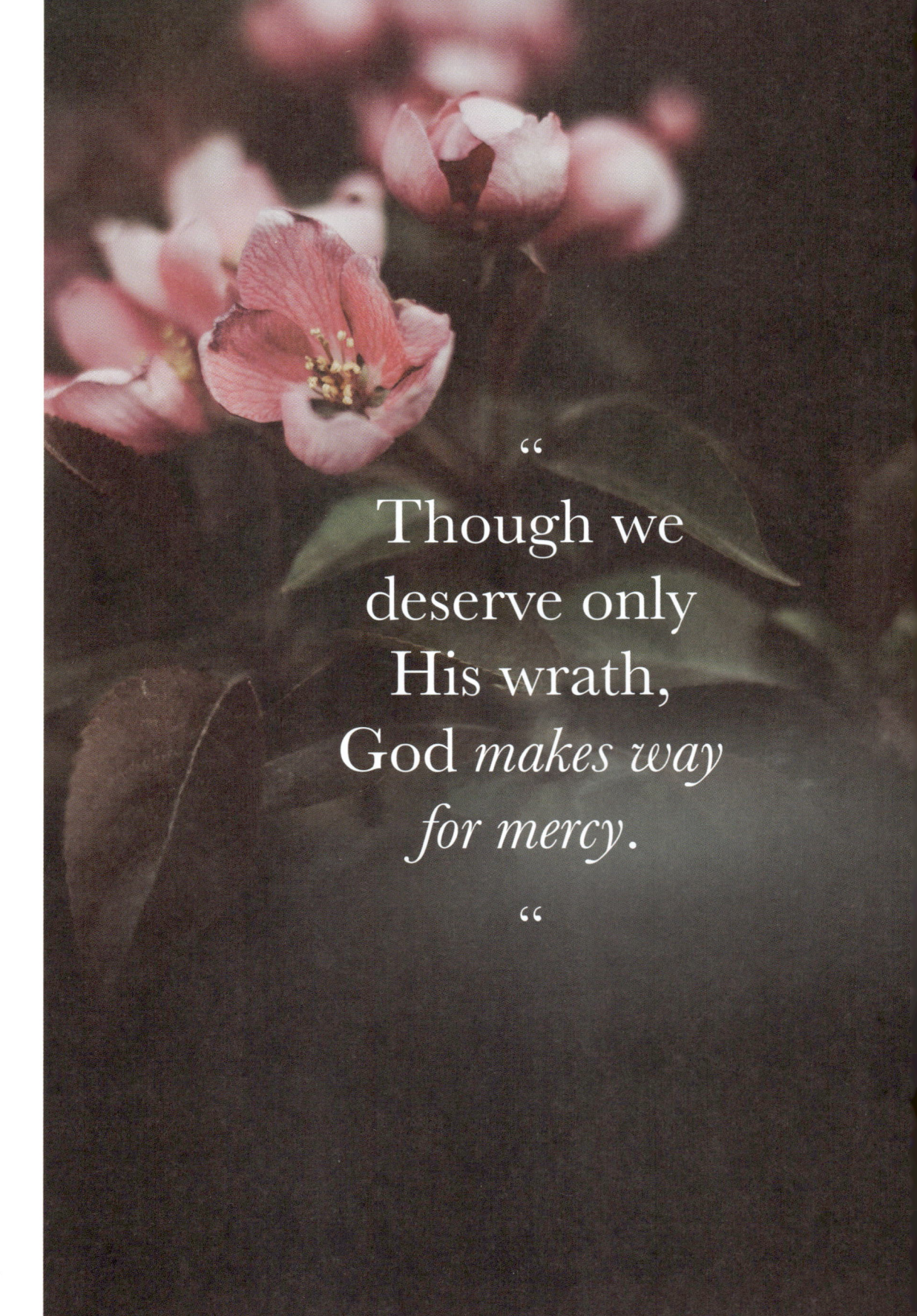

"
Though we deserve only His wrath, God *makes way for mercy.*
"

Merciful

Read Philippians 3:7-10

God is merciful, withholding from us the wrath that we deserve. Whereas grace is God giving us what we do not deserve, God's mercy is Him not giving us what we do deserve. Though all of humanity has fallen short of the glory of God (Romans 3:23) and deserves the penalty of death, God extends mercy. Though we deserve only His wrath, God makes way for mercy. Furthermore, the mercy of God is not a whim or a mood. It is the everlasting and steadfast compassion of God. This mercy is never-changing and unfailing. His mercy is who He is.

Many theologians have pointed to the distinction between God's general mercy and His special mercy. His general mercy is the mercy given to all of humanity. Because we are all sinners deserving of death, each breath we take is an act of God's mercy. He shows believers and unbelievers mercy each day of their lives. In contrast, God's special mercy is that mercy that is given only to the children of God. It is the mercy of salvation and forgiveness. This mercy is eternal and abiding. The mercy of God is a sovereign mercy as displayed throughout Scripture in passages like Romans 9:15. While we do not understand the intricacies of this sovereign mercy, we rest in His character and sovereignty.

Though humans can display mercy, our mercy is limited and finite. Our mercy runs out, and our compassion fails, but the mercy of God is altogether different. It extends to the darkest places offering gentle compassion to sinners far from God.

In considering what it means to be merciful, our greatest example is Jesus. Mercy is one characteristic that is most used to describe Jesus's life on earth. He was often moved with compassion for those whom He encountered. He showed mercy for their physical and spiritual conditions. Yet, there is no place where the mercy of God shines brighter than the cross of Calvary. It is at the cross that mercy and justice meet. The price of our sin and the penalty that we owed had to be paid. However, instead of the debt being paid with our own lives, Jesus paid it with His. He offered up Himself in an act of mercy. He withheld the punishment that we deserved in compassion, grace, and love. God's righteous justice and wrath were fully satisfied because our debt was paid on the cross.

The call of the Christian life is to show mercy as God has shown us mercy. We reflect the mercy of God when we choose to extend mercy to those who do not deserve it. This does not mean that we should put ourselves in an abusive situation, but it does mean demonstrating God's character in our hearts, thoughts, and actions with wisdom. We are called to show mercy as God has so compassionately shown mercy to us.

God is merciful, withholding from us the wrath that we deserve. Whereas grace is God giving us what we do not deserve, God's mercy is Him not giving us what we do deserve.

How have you seen God's mercy in your own life?

How is God's mercy a comfort to you?

Who is someone that you need to extend mercy to right now?

WEEK FIVE *day three*

> "The gospel is a message *of grace*."

Gracious

Read Psalm 103:8-14, Psalm 145:8, Ephesians 1:3-10, 2 Peter 3:17-18

God is gracious, giving us gifts and benefits of which we are undeserving. Grace is a beautiful expression of the steadfast and enduring love of God that pulls us from the depths of our sin and lavishes us with good gifts that we do not deserve. We do not and cannot earn the grace of God. It is bestowed upon us while we are yet sinners without us ever asking for it, wanting it, or desiring it. God's grace comes to undeserving sinners, not because of anything good they have done but because of who God is. He is a God of grace.

In mercy, God withholds from us the punishment that we deserve and places that punishment on Jesus Christ, His Son. In grace, God gives us what we do not deserve. He lavishes us with goodness and blessing that we did not earn. God gives the blessings and righteous standing of the Son of God though we did nothing to deserve these good gifts. These truths intertwine with God's perfect justice and divine love.

The word "grace" is mentioned often, as it should be. Yet, sadly, this has sometimes meant that the richness of grace has become commonplace to us as believers. Grace should never be commonplace. It should leave us in awe and wonder of who our God is, that He would lavish us in a grace that we do not deserve.

The gospel is a message of grace. It is the message of God's abounding grace coming to undeserving sinners, not because of anything good inside them or anything good that they have done but simply because God chose, before the foundations of the world, to lavish them in His limitless love and overflowing grace. The message of the gospel is all about the grace that is found in the person of Jesus Christ and demonstrated for us on the cross.

Jesus perfectly displays grace for us. John 1:17 explains that grace and truth have come through Jesus Christ. This grace is not simply seen in the New Testament, though; God's grace through Jesus has been God's plan since before time began. Ephesians 1 describes God's people as chosen in Him before time began. God's marvelous grace comes through the person and work of Jesus and is given to the children of God.

As we reflect on the grace of God, we must stand in awe of who God is. We come to Him in adoration for all that He has done in us and for us through Jesus. God's grace demands a response from us. When we have truly experienced God's grace, we will never be the same. We cannot simply go back to the way things once were. God also calls us to grow in grace (2 Peter 3:17-18). Through the process of sanctification, we grow in the grace that has been lavished on us. Through our sanctification and growing in grace, we depend on God moment by moment, and we are able to extend grace to those around us as God has extended grace to us.

Grace is a beautiful expression of the steadfast and enduring love of God that pulls us from the depths of our sin and lavishes us with good gifts that we do not deserve.

How have you seen God's grace demonstrated in your life?

What are some practical ways that you can grow in grace?

Write out a prayer, thanking God for the grace He has given you.

day three QUESTIONS

WEEK FIVE *day four*

"
The Lord knows that *He is the only thing* that will satisfy our longing hearts.
"

Jealous

Read Exodus 20:5, Deuteronomy 4:23-24, Joshua 24:19, Isaiah 42:8

God is jealous. He is desirous of receiving the praise and affection He rightly deserves. God is jealous, but He is not jealous in the way that humans are jealous. His jealousy is not selfish or sinful, as is so often the case in humanity's jealousy. His jealousy is not bitter, and it does not harm others. God is jealous for truth and righteousness. Above all, God is jealous for His own glory.

In His jealousy, God displays His wrath over sin, and yet His jealousy is also displayed in love, mercy, grace, and compassion in rescuing sinners and bringing them to Himself. The jealousy of God is not in opposition to His other attributes. From our human perspective, it is hard to understand how jealousy and grace co-exist because we view things from a human lens tainted by sin. God is completely separate from us and untouched by sin and the fall. His jealousy is far different than the jealousy we experience as people.

Many people picture the God of the Old Testament as a God of wrath and jealousy. They separate this picture from their views of Jesus in the New Testament, where He is seen as a God of love and mercy. But the God of the New Testament is the God of the Old Testament. Both the Old and New Testaments explore the themes of God's righteous jealousy and abounding grace.

The jealousy of God is for our good as believers. The Lord knows that He is the only thing that will satisfy our longing hearts. He is jealous for His glory, and He knows that it is also what is best for us. We find meaning in lives that are lived for His glory and not our own. All other pursuits are empty and will leave us searching and longing for something more. God's jealousy for His glory points us back to the source of our joy which is Him alone. Every moment of a believer's life should be lived for the glory of God. This is where joy is found.

The jealousy of God is displayed perfectly in Jesus. John 2:13-22 shows Jesus's jealousy for the glory of God and His wrath over those who had perverted the temple, which was meant to be a place of holy worship. The jealousy of God is also displayed on the cross when Jesus laid down His life for the glory of God and the salvation of His people.

The jealousy of God compels us to a life of service to our King. It moves us to live for His glory and not our own. It reminds us that what matters in this life is His steadfast love, which pursues us when we sin and calls us to repentance and faith. The jealousy of God enables us to live a life free from fear as we rest in God's sovereign pursuit of His glory. The jealousy of God is not something that should cause us uncertainty; it is something in which we should delight.

> *In His jealousy, God displays His wrath over sin, and yet His jealousy is also displayed in love, mercy, grace, and compassion in rescuing sinners and bringing them to Himself.*

Why do you think jealousy is an attribute that makes people feel uncomfortable?

How is God's jealousy a good thing?

How can you live for the glory of God this week?

day four QUESTIONS

WEEK FIVE *day five*

> "God is *patient* because God is *sovereign*."

Patient

Read Exodus 34:6, Nehemiah 9:17, Psalm 86:15, Romans 2:4, 2 Peter 3:9

God is patient. He is long-suffering and enduring. He gives ample opportunity for people to turn toward Him. God's patience is closely tied to His goodness and mercy, yet it is a distinct attribute that marks who God is and how He relates to humanity. His patience is not simply something that He does, but it is who He is.

Patience is hard for us to understand because, frankly, we just do not have much of it. We order packages with same-day shipping, and we become frustrated when a video buffers or a website is slow to load. But God is far different from us. The Scriptures are filled with the pronouncement of God's patience. From His patience in the days of Noah to His long-suffering with the people of Israel, God's interactions with sinners are marked with His patience. He is slow to anger. He abounds in love. He patiently waits while calling sinners to repentance. His patience is strength; it is not weakness. He waits patiently because He is utterly in control. In mercy and love, He patiently waits and pleads for sinners to turn to Him.

God is patient because God is sovereign. He is not worried about what will take place. He is not caught off guard by the events that unfold. He is completely in control, and He already knows what will be. In our desire to control, we rush to action and rarely exhibit patience. Despite our efforts, we are not in control, and we never were. God is thoroughly in control, yet He patiently bears with us and calls us to Himself. He is patient even in our sin and weakness. And in love, He uses these things for His glory.

Jesus is the demonstration of God's patience to us. Jesus patiently lived on this earth for 33 years to accomplish the mission that the Father gave Him. He patiently preached the gospel of the kingdom. He patiently lived with the limitations of humanity. He patiently endured the torment of the cross in our place and loved us while we were yet sinners. Now, Jesus stands in our place as our mediator. Despite our sin and weakness, Jesus pleads with the Father on our behalf and declares us righteous as He clothes us in His righteousness.

The Christian life should be characterized by patience. Patience on this journey is fruit from the Spirit's work in us (Galatians 5:22-

23). We press on in perseverance and faithfulness, and all the while, He is patient with us each time we stumble and each time we fail. His patience for His children never runs out but flows to us like an ever-present stream. How often we take this patience and grace for granted. How often we fail to even notice His patience with us. This patience should indeed lead us to repentance. It should call us to Him over and over again. As we press on in faith, we wait patiently for the day of His coming and the coming of His kingdom here on earth. We look to future glory and a day when all sorrow will be erased, and we will see His face.

He is slow to anger. He abounds in love. He patiently waits while calling sinners to repentance. His patience is strength; it is not weakness. He waits patiently because He is utterly in control.

How have you seen God's patience evidenced in your life?

In what areas of life are you tempted not to have patience?

What sin does a lack of patience reveal?

day five QUESTIONS

WEEK FIVE
Scripture Memory

*But grow in the grace and knowledge
of our Lord and Savior Jesus Christ.
To him be the glory both now and
to the day of eternity.*

2 PETER 3:18

week five REFLECTION
Review all passages from the week

Summarize the main points from this week's Scripture readings.

What did you observe from this week's passages about God and His character?

What do this week's passages reveal about the condition of mankind and yourself?

How do these passages point to the gospel?

How should you respond to these Scriptures? What specific action steps can you take this week to apply them in your life?

Write a prayer in response to your study of God's Word. Adore God for who He is, confess sins He revealed in your own life, ask Him to empower you to walk in obedience, and pray for anyone who comes to mind as you study.

WEEK SIX *day one*

"*Scripture* is wisdom for us."

Wise

Read Isaiah 46:9-10, Isaiah 55:9, Proverbs 3:19, 1 Corinthians 1:20-25, James 1:5, James 3:15-18

God is wise. He is omniscient and judiciously applies His knowledge. More than that, God's wisdom is pure, gentle, and peace-loving (James 3:15-18). His wisdom is also unlike human wisdom. Humans are often thought to grow wiser with years of age and experience. But this is different from the wisdom of God. He did not gather His wisdom over the years and through experiences. While human wisdom is often gained through making mistakes, our God has never made a mistake. There is nothing that He has ever done that was not wise. Wisdom flows from Him because He is wise.

Wisdom is not merely knowledge, but it is the application of knowledge. And in Scripture, wisdom is contrasted with folly (Proverbs 14:8, Proverbs 28:26). Folly means that one lacks good sense and lives foolishly. However, we can rest assured that there is no folly in our God. In a world full of folly, He is wholly wise in all that He does.

The wisdom of God is tied to many of His attributes. From His love to His wrath to His mercy, everything that God does is robed in His majestic wisdom. We can trust that God's patience, faithfulness, and jealousy, are for the best because God never acts in a way that is not wise. He wisely applies His infinite and unlimited knowledge to every sphere of life and every molecule on earth. He is trustworthy, and His wisdom is true.

The wisdom of God does not always make sense to the world around us. And 1 Corinthians 1:20-25 even points out that to the world, the wisdom of God is often seen as foolishness. Yet to the children of God, we find hope in the gospel of our all-wise God. We can see this attribute perfectly displayed in Jesus. Scripture even describes Him as "the wisdom of God" (1 Corinthians 1:24). Though the message of the cross and the gospel of Jesus Christ do not make sense to the world, they are the wisdom of God on display.

The wisdom that we need is found on the pages of God's Word. Scripture is wisdom for us. We must resist the temptation to look to Scripture for knowledge for knowledge's sake. Instead, we need to wisely apply the truth of God's Word to our life. Furthermore, we must fear the Lord because Scripture tells us repeatedly that the fear of the Lord is the beginning of knowledge (Proverbs 9:10). And we must allow the Word of Truth to dwell in us with all wisdom (Colossians 3:16). God has given us wisdom in His Word, and He has given us Himself.

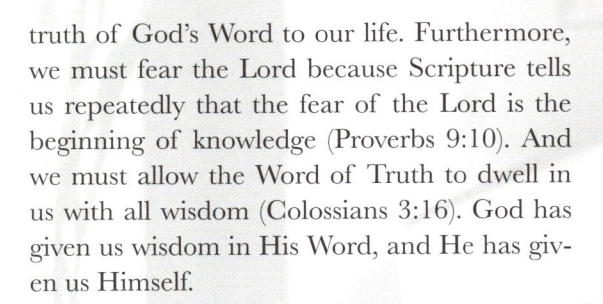

The wisdom of God gives us confidence. It helps us have faith in God, who is working all things for our good, and persevere in the life of faith even when life is confusing and hard. We rest in His unshakable wisdom.

From His love to His wrath to His mercy, everything that God does is robed in His majestic wisdom. We can trust that God's patience, faithfulness, and jealousy, are for the best because God never acts in a way that is not wise.

How is God's wisdom different from man's wisdom?

Read Proverbs 9:10. What do you think it means that the fear of the Lord is the beginning of wisdom?

Why is God's Word essential for us to have wisdom?

day one QUESTIONS

WEEK SIX *day two*

"*Faithfulness* is the story that the Bible tells."

Faithful

Read Numbers 23:19, Deuteronomy 7:9, Lamentations 3:22-23, 2 Timothy 2:13, Hebrews 10:23

God is faithful. God is incapable of anything but fidelity. He is loyally devoted to His plan and purpose. People will let us down, but God never will. We can trust Him to do what He has promised. He can be trusted to be unwavering, unchanging, and ever faithful.

Faithfulness is the story that the Bible tells. From the first chapters in Genesis that promised a Redeemer would come to rescue the people of God from the hopelessness of sin, the Bible tells the story of a faithful God pursuing His own. It tells the story of a God who has covenanted Himself to His people in love so that He could redeem them from the chains of their sin. It is the story of a faithful God pursuing people plagued with unfaithfulness and sin. It is a story of faithfulness from beginning to end.

Over and over again, Scripture teaches that God does what He says. It teaches that He is true to His Word. It shows that He keeps His promises. We can trust Him because He is faithful. Even the world around us declares His faithfulness each day as the sun rises each morning and sets each evening. Every breath that we take is a marker of His faithfulness to us. The fact that we are allowed to go on though we sin against Him every day is a banner of His never-ending faithfulness, mercy, and grace to His children.

Faithfulness is the story of the Bible, and it is our story as well. His faithfulness to us marks our lives. Even our trials and tribulations are used to show us His faithfulness, though we may not understand right away how God will use even our hardest moments and deepest pains for our good and His glory. As we stand in this moment in time, we can look back on His faithfulness and anticipate His faithfulness in our lives. And even beyond our lives, we can trust that He will be faithful. We have the confident hope and expectation of future glory. Jesus will return and make all things new. He will wipe away every tear from our eyes and will dwell with us forever.

Jesus is the ultimate demonstration of God's faithfulness. He is the answer to every promise and the fulfillment of every covenant. Every promise of Scripture points to Jesus as the answer to our souls' longing and the sin that inflicts us. God promised to send a redeemer, and in Jesus, He did just that (Isaiah 42:1-4, Matthew 12:15-21).

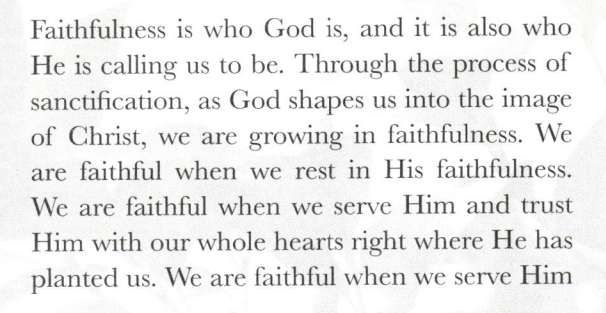

Faithfulness is who God is, and it is also who He is calling us to be. Through the process of sanctification, as God shapes us into the image of Christ, we are growing in faithfulness. We are faithful when we rest in His faithfulness. We are faithful when we serve Him and trust Him with our whole hearts right where He has planted us. We are faithful when we serve Him and love Him even when we do not understand. We are faithful when we persevere as He carries us along through every moment of our lives. We cling to the faithfulness of God in the good days and the bad because we know that He will never leave us or forsake us.

From the first chapters in Genesis that promised a Redeemer would come to rescue the people of God from the hopelessness of sin, the Bible tells the story of a faithful God pursuing His own.

How is the Bible the story of God's faithfulness?

How have you seen God's faithfulness in your own life?

How can you grow in faithfulness?
Where do you struggle to trust and obey?

day two QUESTIONS

WEEK SIX *day three*

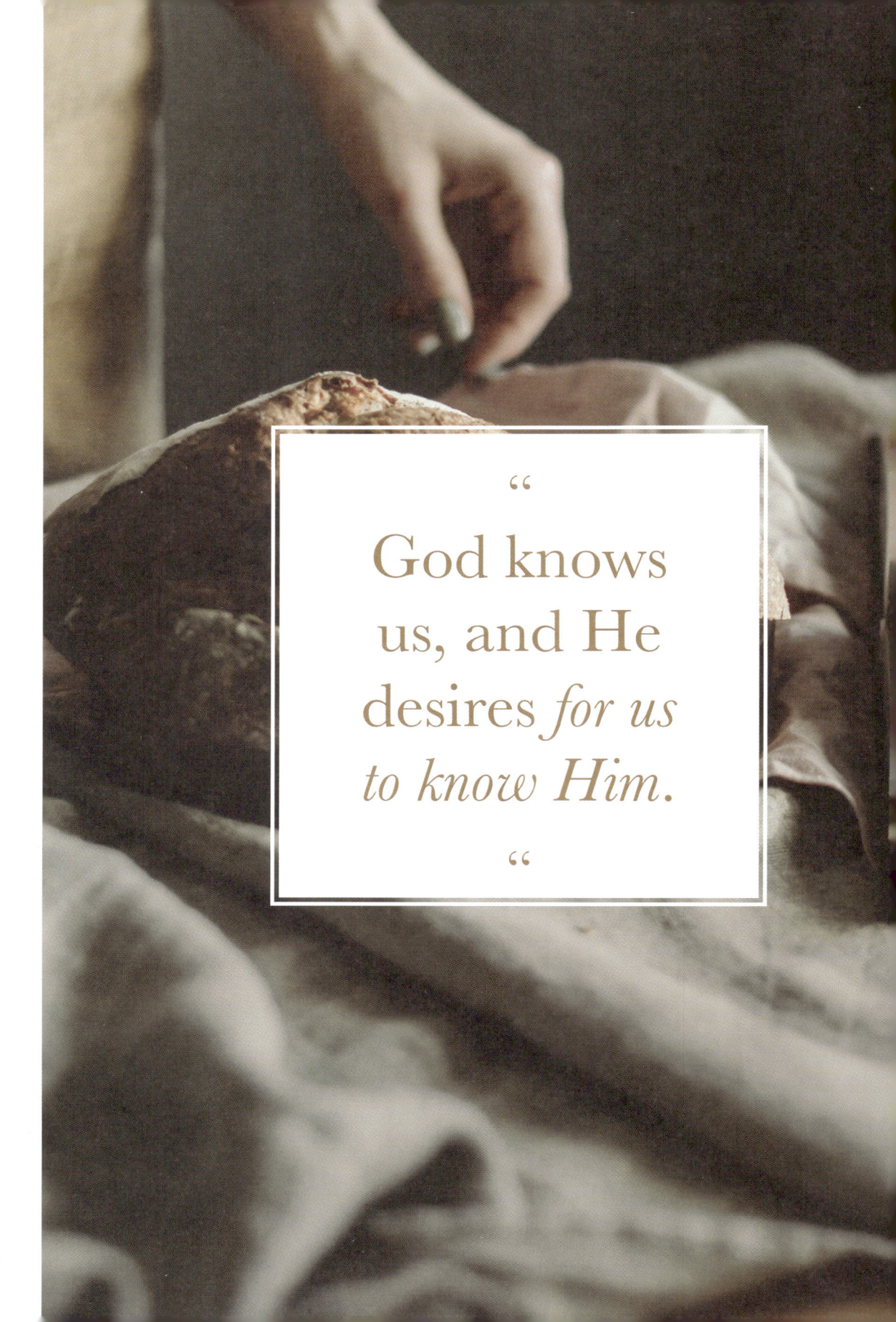

"God knows us, and He desires *for us* to know Him."

How Can We Know God?

Read John 1:1-18, 2 Peter 3:18

As we discussed in week one, day two of this study, knowing God is not just knowing about God. This concept is so important that it bears repeating. There is great value in academic understanding of the Bible and of understanding the deep riches of theology. However, as we previously discussed, if we only ever know about God without knowing Him, we have missed the point. This danger of knowing about God but not knowing Him is not limited to an academic context, though. Many have grown up in the church or had a basic understanding of Christianity without ever knowing God. If we only ever know about God, we have missed the point of the gospel. Jesus did not come so that we could know about Him but so that we could know Him.

How do we know God, and how does He reveal Himself to us? We do not need to look far to see the evidence of how God reveals Himself to us. Through general revelation, God reveals Himself through the world around us. Every sunrise declares His faithfulness, and every sunset proclaims His glory. Every breath that we take demonstrates His sustaining power over all things. We see His creativity in the beautiful world in which we live. His attributes are displayed in the world around us, and even in His people, we see glimpses of His character.

The world around us proclaims that God exists and declares His glory, and yet there is something more that we need in order to understand the beauty of the gospel. Through special revelation, we see the hope of salvation. This is God's Word and Jesus Himself. Through the pages of Scripture, God reveals Himself to us. Every word points to who He is and points to the gospel of Jesus Christ. It is far too easy for us to be complacent about the Bible that we hold in our hands. Even if we regularly read and study it, we can forget to marvel at the gift that it is. The Word of God that we hold in our hands reveals the heart of God. It tells us who He is and shows us how He loves us. May we never get over the gift that it is to us. God wants us to know Him and glorify Him, which is why He has given us His Word.

The mystery of the incarnation reveals God to us. The incarnation is the truth that God Himself became a man in Jesus. God the Son came as a helpless baby to show us God's heart of love and His relentless pursuit of His own. Jesus experienced what we experience and sympathizes with our weakness. Jesus gave up heaven's glory to humble Himself for our salvation. He lived the perfect life that we could never have lived, no matter how hard we tried. He went to the cross and died the death that we deserved so that we could be made sons and daughters of God. And the hope of the gospel is that Jesus did this while we were sinners far from Him. He did this for His own so that we could know Him. He pursued us in love and grace when we would never have searched for Him. In Jesus, we see all the attributes of God in the flesh.

God knows us, and He desires for us to know Him. He wants us to see Him everywhere we look. And most of all, He wants us to see Him in His Word and in His Son, who is the Word made flesh (John 1:14). The more we know Him, the more we will love Him. The more we read His Word, the more we will love His Word. The more we seek Him, the more we will find Him because He has sought, loved, and known us first.

Through the pages of Scripture, God reveals Himself to us. Every word points to who He is and points to the gospel of Jesus Christ.

How is knowing God different than knowing about God?

How does Jesus show us who God is?

How can you pursue knowing God more this week?

day three QUESTIONS

WEEK SIX *day four*

"We were created to *know God*."

Knowing Him and Being Known By Him

Read Jeremiah 9:23-24, John 17:3, Philippians 3:10, 2 Peter 3:18

We were created to know God. It is our greatest goal and our highest calling. As His disciples, God made us to be students of who He is. And the study of the attributes of God is all about knowing Him. We do not examine His character for academic knowledge. We study who He is because we desire to know Him.

We cannot understand who we are apart from understanding God, who made us in His image and has created us for His glory. When we study God's attributes, we see how we fall short of God's righteousness, which leaves us humbled and grateful that our perfect God pursued our imperfect hearts. This shows us our worth and how much we are loved. Finally, when we study God's attributes, we grow in our love for God, and through His mysterious power, our hearts are transformed. As He changes our hearts, we also understand the world around us. We begin to see others through the eyes of God and share in His wrath for injustice and mercy for the undeserving.

Furthermore, when we study God's attributes, we understand that God knows us. He knows our sins and weaknesses. He knows our misplaced motives and the bitterness that can so easily arise in our souls. He knows our frustration when we seek to follow Him and find ourselves falling into sin again. He holds every tear, and He weeps with us in our suffering. He is moved with compassion, and our names are written on His hands (Isaiah 49:16). We are His—fully known and fully loved, though we deserve nothing but wrath.

We find glory in who He is and in the cross of Christ. Jeremiah 9:23-24 points us to the truth that our greatest achievement is not our wisdom or riches but in knowing the Lord and understanding His ways. The world around us will try to define success for us. But success is knowing Him and doing what He has called us to do. More than that, knowing Him is worth far more than this world could ever offer us.

In Jesus, God sympathizes with us. He understands the weakness of our humanity because He humbled Himself to take on flesh. The God of creation left heaven's throne to become a helpless baby, and in doing so, He sympathized with our vulnerable state. He walked the earth and was not immune to life's pains in a fallen world or the effects of sin's curse. He knew sadness and betrayal, yet He went to the cross in our place. And the only way that we can know God and be known by God is because Jesus came to rescue us from the domain of darkness to bring us into His light.

He calls those who are weary and burdened with anxiety to come to Him and find rest for their souls (Matthew 11:28-29). It is in coming to Him and knowing Him through His Word that we find rest for our weary souls and hope for our wounded hearts.

He knows His own. We know Him and love Him only because He knew and loved us first. We run to Him only because He ran to us first. Now our lives should be poured out as an offering to Him. This means that we should submit our lives to Christ and honor Him in all that we do to glorify His name. He is good, faithful, and true. Every day of our lives should be dedicated to knowing and loving Him more. And every day of our lives, as children of God, we rest securely, understanding that we are known, and the Maker of the universe loves us.

*We cannot understand who we are
apart from understanding God,
who made us in His image and has
created us for His glory.*

What does it mean to truly know God?

How should knowing God transform your life?

Read Jeremiah 9:23-24. In what things are you tempted to boast?

day four QUESTIONS

> "Reflecting God's attributes is about *daily dependence*."

Reflecting God's Attributes

Read Genesis 1:27, Psalm 86:11, Ephesians 5:1-2, 1 Peter 2:21, 1 John 2:6

God made us in His image. We have been created in His likeness to reflect who He is. As God's redeemed children, we now live to not only know who God is but also to reflect His character. The Christian life is a journey of knowing God more and growing into His likeness day by day.

The incommunicable attributes such as God's sovereignty, omnipotence, and omniscience are reserved for God alone. These are not things that we as humans can or should seek to emulate. But the communicable attributes such as God's love, mercy, and patience are things that we should continually practice and develop as we grow in sanctification and holiness.

We were made to know God, and we were made to reflect His image to the world around us. When we do these things, we fulfill our purpose, as the Westminster Catechism states, "to glorify God and enjoy Him forever." When we know Him, we will be compelled to glorify Him. And it is in knowing Him that we can more fully find joy and satisfaction in who He is. Theology is the study of God and is not just for pastors or seminary students. The study of God is for every believer. The most practical thing we can do is pursue an understanding of who He is. Understanding God's character also helps us understand ourselves. In turn, we see why He made us and how He desires us to grow in His grace.

We study God's attributes to know Him, and the more we know Him, the more we are humbled by who He is, repentant over our sin, and sanctified by His grace. This process of sanctification makes us more and more like God. This is good news because we should bear a striking resemblance to our Father as children of God.

We look to Jesus to understand what it means to live out the attributes of God. We look to Him to know what it means for those attributes to be displayed in humanity. And, we look to Jesus for His transforming power and the hope of a future day when our sanctification will be complete (Philippians 1:6).

Reflecting God's attributes is not about trying harder and doing better in our own strength. It is not about a checklist of New Year's resolutions that we will aimlessly try to live up to. No, reflecting God's attributes is about knowing Him and being fashioned by His gentle hands into what He has called us to be. Reflecting God's attributes is about daily dependence. It is about understanding how we fall short and how He completes in us what He has called us to be. He is the one who saves, and He is the one who sanctifies. In light of God's attributes, our lives should overflow with awe at who He is and gratitude for how He has pursued us.

> *As God's redeemed children, we now live to not only know who God is but also to reflect His character. The Christian life is a journey of knowing God more and growing into His likeness day by day.*

What attributes stood out to you most in this study?

What attribute do you need to ask God to help you reflect today?

How should the study of God's attributes impact the way that we live?

day five QUESTIONS

WEEK SIX
Scripture Memory

Teach me your way, Lord, and I will live by your truth. Give me an undivided mind to fear your name.

—

PSALM 86:11

week six REFLECTION
Review all passages from the week

Summarize the main points from this week's Scripture readings.

What did you observe from this week's passages about God and His character?

What do this week's passages reveal about the condition of mankind and yourself?

How do these passages point to the gospel?

How should you respond to these Scriptures? What specific action steps can you take this week to apply them in your life?

Write a prayer in response to your study of God's Word. Adore God for who He is, confess sins He revealed in your own life, ask Him to empower you to walk in obedience, and pray for anyone who comes to mind as you study.

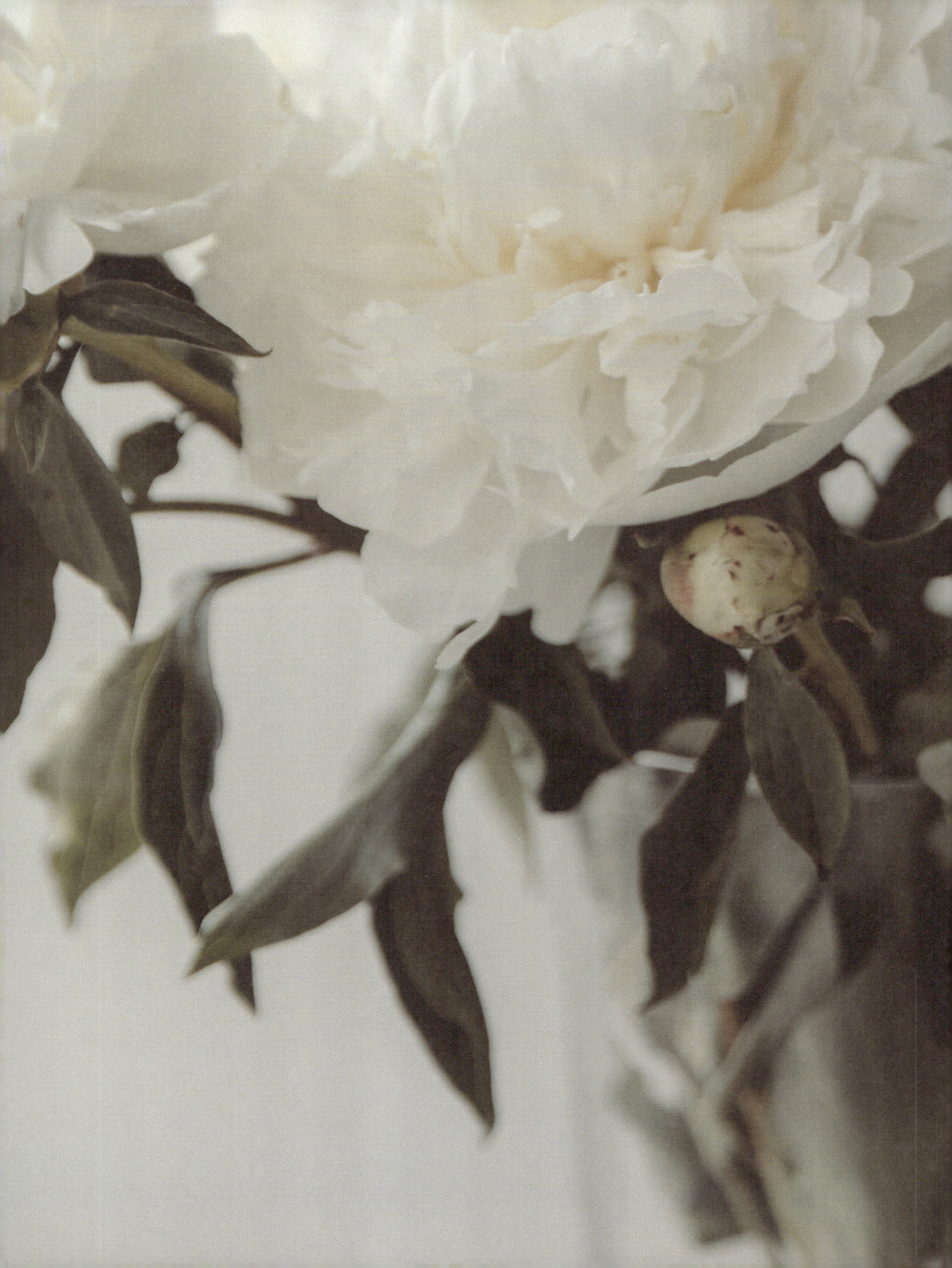

THE ATTRIBUTES OF GOD

Scripture Reference Guide

ETERNAL

Psalm 90
Isaiah 41:4, 46:9-10
Habakkuk 1:12
Hebrews 13:8
Revelation 1:4, 8

FAITHFUL

Numbers 23:19
Deuteronomy 7:9
Lamentations 3:22-23
2 Timothy 2:13
Hebrews 10:23

GOOD

Genesis 1:31
Psalm 25:8-9, 34:8, 100:5, 107, 119:68
Nahum 1:7

GRACIOUS

2 Kings 13:23
Psalm 103:8-14, 145:8
Ephesians 1:3-10
2 Peter 3:17-18

HOLY

Exodus 15:11
Leviticus 19:2
Isaiah 6:3
Psalm 29:1-2
Habakkuk 1:13
Ephesians 1:4-6
1 Peter 1:15
Revelation 4:8

IMMUTABLE

1 Samuel 15:29
Psalm 19:14, 33:11, 90:2, 102:26-28
Malachi 3:6
Romans 11:29
Hebrews 13:8
James 1:17

INCOMPREHENSIBLE AND TRANSCENDENT

Psalm 145:3
Isaiah 40:12-18, 46:9-11, 55:8-9
Romans 11:33-36

INFINITE

Psalm 147:5
Isaiah 40:28
Romans 11:33-36
2 Corinthians 12:9-10

JEALOUS

Exodus 20:5
Deuteronomy 4:23-24
Joshua 24:19
Isaiah 42:8

JUST

Genesis 18:25
Deuteronomy 32:3-4
Psalm 9:7-8, 89:14, 146:7-9
Isaiah 61:8
Micah 6:8
Romans 3:26

LOVING

Exodus 34:6-7
Psalm 136
Isaiah 54:10
John 3:16
Romans 5:1-8
Galatians 2:20
Ephesians 2:4-5
1 John 4:16

MERCIFUL

Psalm 145:9
Lamentations 3:22-24
Luke 6:36
2 Corinthians 1:3
Ephesians 2:4-5
Titus 3:5
1 Peter 1:3

OMNIPOTENT

Job 26:14, 42:1-2
Psalm 33:8-9, 147:5
Jeremiah 32:17, 27
Matthew 19:26
Luke 1:37
Ephesians 3:16-21

OMNIPRESENT

1 Kings 8:27
Psalm 139:7-10
Proverbs 15:3
Jeremiah 23:23-24
Colossians 1:15-20

OMNISCIENT

- Psalm 139:1-4, 147:4
- Isaiah 40:27-28
- Romans 11:33-36
- Hebrews 4:13
- 1 John 3:20

PATIENT

- Exodus 34:6
- Nehemiah 9:17
- Psalm 86:15
- Romans 2:4
- 2 Peter 3:9

SELF-EXISTENT

- Psalm 90:1-2
- John 1:1-4, 5:26
- Acts 17:28

SELF-SUFFICIENT

- Isaiah 40:28-31
- Acts 17:24-25
- Philippians 4:19
- Hebrews 1:1-4

SOVEREIGN

- 1 Chronicles 29:11-12
- Job 23:13
- Psalm 24:1-2
- Isaiah 14:24
- Daniel 4:34-35
- Romans 9:14-16
- Ephesians 1
- Colossians 1:17
- Revelation 4:11

TRUTHFUL

- Numbers 23:19
- Psalm 119:160
- Isaiah 45:19
- John 1:14, 3:33, 14:6
- Romans 1:25
- Hebrews 6:18-19
- 1 John 5:20

WISE

- Proverbs 3:19
- Isaiah 46:9-10, 55:9
- 1 Corinthians 1:20-25
- James 1:5, 3:15-18

WRATHFUL

- Psalm 69:24, 147:11
- Nahum 1:2-6
- John 3:36
- Romans 1:18
- Revelation 19:15

The attributes of God reveal three things. They reveal to us *His character, our sin,* and *the glorious gospel.*

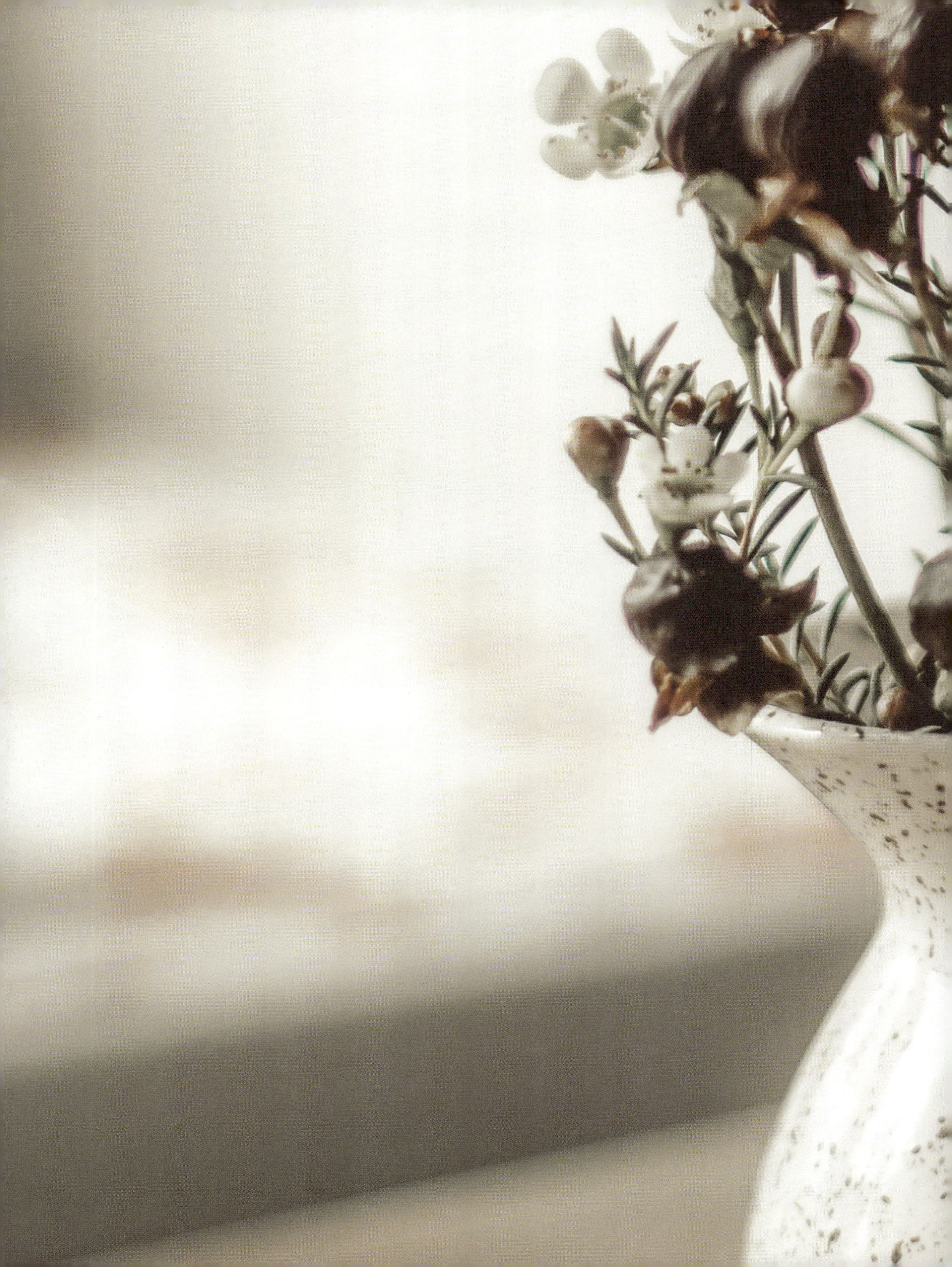

The story of
Scripture declares
who God is.

What is the Gospel?

THANK YOU FOR READING AND ENJOYING THIS STUDY WITH US! WE ARE ABUNDANTLY GRATEFUL FOR THE WORD OF GOD, THE INSTRUCTION WE GLEAN FROM IT, AND THE EVER-GROWING UNDERSTANDING IT PROVIDES FOR US OF GOD'S CHARACTER. WE ARE ALSO THANKFUL THAT SCRIPTURE CONTINUALLY POINTS TO ONE THING IN INNUMERABLE WAYS: THE GOSPEL.

We remember our brokenness when we read about the fall of Adam and Eve in the garden of Eden (Genesis 3), when sin entered into a perfect world and maimed it. We remember the necessity that something innocent must die to pay for our sin when we read about the atoning sacrifices in the Old Testament. We read that we have all sinned and fallen short of the glory of God (Romans 3:23) and that the penalty for our brokenness, the wages of our sin, is death (Romans 6:23). We all are in need of grace and mercy, but most importantly, we all need a Savior.

We consider the goodness of God when we realize that He did not plan to leave us in this dire state. We see His promise to buy us back from the clutches of sin and death in Genesis 3:15. And we see that promise accomplished with Jesus Christ on the cross. Jesus Christ knew no sin yet became sin so that we might become righteous through His sacrifice (2 Corinthians 5:21). Jesus was tempted in every way that we are and lived sinlessly. He was reviled yet still yielded Himself for our sake, that we may have life abundant in Him. Jesus lived the perfect life that we could not live and died the death that we deserved.

The gospel is profound yet simple. There are many mysteries in it that we will never understand this side of heaven, but there is still overwhelming weight to its implications in this life. The gospel tells of our sinfulness and God's goodness and a gracious gift that compels a response. We are saved by grace through faith, which means that we rest with faith in the grace that Jesus Christ displayed on the cross (Ephesians 2:8-9). We cannot save ourselves from our brokenness or do any amount of good works to merit God's favor, but we can have faith that what Jesus accomplished in His death, burial, and resurrection was more than enough for our salvation and our eternal delight. When we accept God, we are commanded to die to ourselves and our sinful desires and live a life worthy of the calling we have received (Ephesians 4:1). The gospel compels us to be sanctified, and in so doing, we are conformed to the likeness of Christ Himself. This is hope. This is redemption. This is the gospel.

SCRIPTURE TO REFERENCE:

GENESIS 3:15 — *I will put hostility between you and the woman, and between your offspring and her offspring. He will strike your head, and you will strike his heel.*

ROMANS 3:23 — *For all have sinned and fall short of the glory of God.*

ROMANS 6:23 — *For the wages of sin is death, but the gift of God is eternal life in Christ Jesus our Lord.*

2 CORINTHIANS 5:21 — *He made the one who did not know sin to be sin for us, so that in him we might become the righteousness of God.*

EPHESIANS 2:8-9 — *For you are saved by grace through faith, and this is not from yourselves; it is God's gift — not from works, so that no one can boast.*

EPHESIANS 4:1 — *Therefore I, the prisoner in the Lord, urge you to walk worthy of the calling you have received,*

Thank you for studying
God's Word with us!

CONNECT WITH US
@thedailygraceco
@dailygracepodcast

CONTACT US
info@thedailygraceco.com

SHARE
#thedailygraceco

VISIT US ONLINE
www.thedailygraceco.com

MORE DAILY GRACE
Daily Grace® Podcast